I0066819

ACCOUNTING IN SMALL
BUSINESS DECISIONS

Small Business Management Research Reports
Prepared by the University of Kentucky for the
Small Business Administration, Washington 25, D.C.

PUBLISHED UNDER THE UNIVERSITY
OF KENTUCKY STUDIES PROGRAM

ACCOUNTING IN SMALL BUSINESS DECISIONS

By JAMES L. GIBSON

Assistant Professor of Business Administration,
Arlington State College

and W. WARREN HAYNES

Professor of Economics, University of Kentucky

Prepared by the UNIVERSITY OF KENTUCKY
under the Small Business Administration
Management Research Grant Program

Project Director: JAMES W. MARTIN
Director, Bureau of Business Research

UNIVERSITY OF KENTUCKY PRESS
Lexington, 1963

Copyright © 1963 by the University of Kentucky Press

University of Kentucky Printing Division
Library of Congress Catalog Card
No. 62-19376

FOREWORD

This study has been conducted and prepared under the direction of James W. Martin, project director for the University of Kentucky. The research was financed by a grant made by the Small Business Administration, United States Government, under the authority of Public Law 699 (85th Congress).

Only a limited number of copies of this report have been printed. It is available for reference in any of the Small Business Administration offices throughout the United States or at many reference libraries. Copies of the report also may be purchased directly from the University of Kentucky Press, Lexington, Kentucky.

Summaries of this study are being printed and will be available in reasonable quantities. These summaries may be secured from SBA field offices or from the Small Business Administration, Washington 25, D. C.

The Small Business Administration assumes no responsibility for the accuracy of the data contained herein, nor does it necessarily endorse any opinions, conclusions, or recommendations which may be a part of this report.

> JOHN E. HORNE
> Administrator
> Small Business Administration

ACKNOWLEDGMENTS

This study results from the efforts of a great many people. We are indebted to the managers of small firms who contributed their time and interest; without their cooperation the descriptive findings could not have been gathered. We are indebted to Bernard Davis, Lawrence Goodman, Robert Haun, Dale Osborne, and Martin Solomon, Jr., who, with us, comprised the research team which collected and analyzed the case studies. James W. Martin's excellent editorial assistance and Mrs. Judy Shewmaker's unsurpassed secretarial skills must be acknowledged. Finally, various members of the University of Kentucky faculty read and commented on early drafts; their attention saved the authors from many errors of logic and detail. We assume full responsibility for any shortcomings of the study which remain.

JAMES L. GIBSON
W. WARREN HAYNES

CONTENTS

FIGURES

INTRODUCTION

$\mathcal{T}HIS$ STUDY attempts to fill a gap in the literature of small business management. Previously there have been few studies—particularly empirical studies on the individual firm—of the role of accounting in small business decisions.[1] There is a body of prescriptive literature in the areas of financial and cost accounting. But, to our knowledge, this is the first large-scale empirical examination of how small firms actually use accounting data in making operating decisions.

This study is concerned simultaneously with prescription and description. It investigates the role accounting can play, seeking to establish norms of reasonable behavior. It also determines the actual practices and the reasons for them. By interrelating the normative and the descriptive, this study attempts to determine the range of the possible; it tries to show what small firms can do within the limitations of staff, finances, and volumes of sales too small to justify large expenditures on special accounting systems. It tries to indicate what better use small firms can make of the data they now have, as well as the use of data that might become available.

The chief findings result from an intensive analysis of approximately 100 case studies of actual small business practices, 44 of which are specifically cited in the text. A research team visited the cooperating firms and interviewed the key executives. These interviews uncovered various types of decisions in a single firm. In almost all of the companies pricing decisions were important; therefore, the research team gave them special attention. A second emphasis was upon investment decisions, e.g., the purchase of a plant, equipment, or inventory. In a few of the firms miscellaneous situations deserved attention, e.g., decisions concerned with liquidation, with changes in the product mix, and with the choice between making and buying an item. Pricing and investment decisions were emphasized because of the opportunity to make a more thorough comparative study of the subjects in the setting of small business than had ever before been undertaken.

The team deliberately did not attempt to obtain a representative sample of firms. Instead it took advantage of the willingness of certain firms to cooperate and of previous contacts with business managers. The managers spoke frankly and provided opportunities for persistent follow-ups. A representative sample would necessarily include firms in which this frankness and cooperation would be more limited. In any case, the study does cover a wide range of small business situations.

[1] See Clinton W. Bennett, "A Case Study of Small Business Controls," N.A.C.A. *Bulletin*, XXIX (April 15, 1948), 991-1026; Harry Hodgson, "Installation of Management Accounting in a Small Business," *Accountant*, CXXXV (July 28, Aug. 4, 1956), 76-9, 111-3; Peter Jardine, "Applications of Management Accounting Techniques to Small Business," *Cost Accountant*, XXXIV (June, 1955), 6-17.

The Small Business Administration's criteria for "small" have been used here. In general, a small business is independently owned and operated and is not dominant in its field of operation. For specific industries, additional criteria are: (1) manufacturing firms must have no more than 500 employees, or in some special cases no more than 1,000; (2) wholesale concerns must have annual receipts of no more than $5 million; (3) retail outlets must have annual receipts of no more than $1 million or in some cases no more than $2 million; (4) service outlets must have annual receipts of no more than $1 million; (5) construction firms must have annual receipts of no more than $5 million; (6) trucking and warehousing firms must have annual receipts of no more than $2 million. One department store (noted in the text) is the only exception to the criteria.

The team avoided structured interviews. A questionnaire would not have allowed so thorough an analysis. This was made clear when the interviewees' initial answers to questions often proved upon more intensive investigation to be superficial. A continual probing into responses was necessary to determine how the firms actually did make their decisions.

1

ACCOUNTING AND ECONOMICS: THEIR
RELATION TO DECISION MAKING

$\mathcal{I}T$ *IS GENERALLY* recognized that both accounting data and logic of economics enter into business decisions. Exactly what their respective contributions are or what they potentially might be is, however, not clearly defined. This chapter attacks the problem of definition, not by an empirical analysis of actual cases but by an *a priori* examination of functions. Accounting provides the data while managerial economics offers a system for handling those data in making decisions; such, roughly, is the nature of the relationship between accounting and economics. This study examines the relationship between accounting and economics in small business firms and evaluates the use these firms do make and can make of accounting data.

ACCOUNTING AND BUSINESS DECISIONS

Traditionally, management decision making has not been a main emphasis of accounting. Financial accounting and cost accounting stress the reporting of a firm's progress and the control of costs. The result has been lack of clarity about what role accounting can play in decisions. Figure 1 shows the relationship between various branches of accounting and their ultimate uses. It suggests that only variable cost systems and nonintegrated cost analyses aim directly at providing data for decisions. Accounting is predominantly used for other purposes. Only in recent years have accountants stressed the uses of accounting in internal management of the firm.

One approach to the role of accounting in business decisions is to examine the decision-making process. This process consists of several steps:

1. Recognition of the need for a decision.
2. Determination of alternative courses of action.
3. Assembly of and organization of relevant information.
4. Evaluation of each alternative.
5. Choice of one of the alternatives.
6. Follow-up of the decision.

The importance of accounting in the last step is clear. Both financial accounting and cost accounting report historical data which aid in following up past decisions. Since a decision looks to the future rather than the past, we are concerned primarily with the part accounting can play in the recognition that a need for a decision exists and the assembly of relevant information.

Recognition of the need for a decision

A decision involves a change from a less desirable po-

Figure 1. A classification of accounting methods with reference
to the ultimate use of the data

| Accounting Methods | Users and Uses of Information | | | | | | | |
| | External | | | | | Internal | | |
	Stockholders	Creditors	Security analysts	Regulatory bodies	Tax authorities	Planning	Control	Decision making
INTEGRATED IN THE GENERAL LEDGER:								
Financial Accounting:								
Statement preparation	1	1	1	1	1	–	–	2
Statement analysis	1	1	1	1	–	2	1	2
Funds analysis	–	1	–	–	–	1	2	2
Subsidiary records keeping	–	1	–	1	2	–	1	2
Cost Accounting:								
Variable cost systems						–	1	1
Absorption:			SEE NOTE					
Historical cost systems						–	1	2
Predetermined cost systems						–	1	2
NOT INTEGRATED:								
Budgeting	–	–	–	–	–	1	1	2
Auditing	1	1	1	1	1	–	1	–
Cost Analysis:								
Programed analysis	–	–	–	–	–	1	1	1
Nonprogramed analysis	–	–	–	–	–	–	–	1

Principal uses are designated by 1; secondary uses, by 2; nonuses, by a dash.

NOTE: Although these techniques develop inventory valuations which are important in the areas served by financial accounting, cost accounting methods emphasize the development of data for internal management uses.

6

sition to one which is more desirable. In order for this change to take place, the present position must be compared with a preconceived notion of what is desirable. Accounting data are important in this phase for they provide the best assessment of the present available to the businessman.

The concept of homeostasis helps describe this kind of behavior. Homeostasis is the tendency of organisms to return to a given structure in the face of changing conditions. Kenneth Boulding has incorporated this idea into the theory of the firm. In his words: "The simplest theory of the firm is to assume that there is a 'homeostasis of the balance sheet'—that there is some desired quantity of all the various items in the balance sheet, and that any disturbance of this structure immediately sets in motion forces which will restore the status quo."[1] Perhaps the emphasis should not be on the status quo but on a moving set of preferences over time. Thus, actual events are continually compared with a dynamically shifting set of standards.

Homeostasis and financial accounting. As Boulding's statement suggests, the accountant's balance sheet stimulates decisions because it reports conditions that can be compared to homeostatic norms. For example, the value of liquid assets may exceed some predetermined criteria of balance. This may lead to a consideration of alternatives such as expansion of facilities or the payment of dividends. The relationship between assets and creditor-owner claims may not be the one that is desired. This condition could lead to liquidation of outstanding debt or to increased debt, depending upon the set of preferences. The balance sheet may not be as important for internal decision making as for external relations with stockholders and creditors; nevertheless, it is a stimulus to action by internal management.

Even more important in stimulating decisions is the income statement. Whether or not the objective is the maximum profit or a satisfactory profit, there is always interest

[1] Kenneth E. Boulding, *A Reconstruction of Economics* (New York: John Wiley & Sons, Inc., 1950), p. 27.

7

in the reported income. As recent studies have revealed, many firms have predetermined notions of desired profit, whether it be called a "target figure," or a "reasonable" profit, or an "adequate" return. The income statement provides the means by which the firm can compare its actual position with its goal. The items in the income statement which, when arranged, give net income can likewise be judged on the basis of predetermined norms. For example, a particular expense item when taken in relation to sales may exceed a set figure and may in turn lead to a determination of alternatives.

More refined analyses of accounting statements such as ratio analysis, common-size statements, and common-dollar statements are direct applications of the idea of homeostasis. The mere fact that such analyses are used indicates that the present situation is being examined with reference to preconceived ideas of acceptability. The use of ratio analysis implies comparison with industry averages, trade association suggestions, or past experience. Common-size statements allow analysis to be made of component items within a statement with reference to the whole. This again shows the concern for desired relationships.

Other financial accounting methods also illustrate the homeostasis concept. Working capital analysis, source and application of funds analysis, and creditor and debtor claims analysis are methods which present information concerning the present state of affairs for comparison with sets of preferences. All of these methods are concerned with balance sheet and income statement items. However, the information is arranged to reveal certain relationships which are not entirely evident in the usual financial statement presentation. The purpose is to make comparisons and discover possible needs for decision making.

Homeostasis and cost accounting. A discussion of cost accounting might include a variety of topics. The present discussion is concerned with the relationship between certain cost accounting techniques and the recognition of the need for decisions. This emphasis directs attention to cost control techniques rather than to the other features of cost accounting. All control techniques incorporate at least these four steps:

1. Information on the actual state of affairs.

2. Comparison of the actual state with a predetermined norm.

3. Determination of the magnitude of any deviation.

4. Action which makes the actual match the predetermined norm.

Standard cost accounting systems integrate to some extent the concept of homeostasis into the ledger. The first phase of decision making (recognizing the need for decision) has been partly routinized. Standard cost systems require a set of preferences for costs and a set of preferences for the amount of deviation that will be tolerated. It is too expensive to revise the standards continually as objectives change, but changed preferences can be taken into account in the analysis of cost variances. For interim operations, the set of preferences is expressed by the tolerable zone of variance. For example, a 10 percent variance or below is tolerated initially; but as the concern for lower costs and increased efficiency intensifies, the tolerable variance may drop to 6 percent. If a variance develops which exceeds management's aim, decision making is activated.

A familiar example of the homeostasis idea is budgeting. Constructing and using a budget requires a set of preferences be established for operations of the entire firm and decisions be stimulated when the budgeted amounts are exceeded.

Assembly and organization of relevant information

Accounting assembles information on alternative courses of action in two ways. The first method attempts to routinize the collection of relevant data and may be called *programed analysis*. The data used in such an analysis may come from general ledger accounts, but are arranged in a form which aids in decision making. The second method is the specific cost study, *nonprogramed analysis*, which develops information for specific decisions. One of the major issues in this volume is the extent to which small businessmen can profit from these two approaches.

There is a wide variety of ways in which data can be organized for decisions. The objective should be to arrange the data in a form that brings simplicity out of complexity, that focuses attention on the most important variables, and that facilitates further analysis. Such arrangements may then lead to further statistical treatment or to subjective evaluations by management. As an illustration, a firm may seek organized data on the sales of various items, arranged by sizes and shapes, in order to help it forecast the sizes and shapes that will be demanded in the future. It may wish sales data organized by territories to indicate where sales are increasing or decreasing. Such arrangements bring out pertinent factors involved in decisions. Probably of greatest interest to the manager of a firm is that arrangement of data which emphasizes the impact of decisions on costs. The most useful analysis for him in this respect, it would seem, involves specifically the incremental costs, i.e., those costs which will be affected by some particular decision.

Programed methods. The following three accounting methods are representative of analyses which provide incremental data systematically. The accounting system can be designed by account classification to generate such data systematically, or as is the usual case, the data can be taken from ordinary financial accounts and rearranged in the form suggested by incremental analysis.

1. *Direct costing* is defined as the segregation of fixed and variable costs.[2] For many management decisions, this segregation is necessary in order to reveal cost-profit-volume relationships. Direct costing identifies only variable costs with products, thus giving management product cost data as a function of output. It should be obvious that this type of

[2] See National Association of Cost Accountants, *Direct Costing,* N.A.C.A. Research Report No. 23, April 1, 1953.

10

routinized accounting method moves in the direction of the incremental approach to decision making.

The allocation of fixed costs to products on some arbitrary basis may result in confusion on some decisions. Direct costing attempts to do away with this possibility by avoiding overhead allocations. Cost information so developed may correspond closely to marginal costs or incremental costs. In fact, to the extent that direct costs and variable costs are synonomous, and to the extent that variable costs approximate marginal cost (in the case of little or no curvature of the total cost function), direct costs are synonomous with marginal costs.

2. *Marginal income analysis* is a routinized approach similar to direct costing.[3] This method is more universally applicable in that it can be applied to any "segment," i.e., cause of costs. Effective use requires that segments be carefully identified and that an accurate distinction be made between the fixed and variable costs of each segment. The basic ideas involved are similar to those in breakeven analysis as shown in figure 2.

In actual use of the analysis, primary emphasis is placed on marginal balances (sales minus variable costs) and marginal income ratios (gross profit to sales). With this type of information flowing systematically to decision makers, decisions can be based on pertinent costs. The analysis aids both shortrun and longrun decisions: shortrun decisions concerning increased or decreased volume require variable cost information; longrun decisions, which involve abandoning the segment, require data on both variable costs and escapable fixed costs.

This method is concerned with the relative contribution of each segment to unassigned fixed costs and profit. No attempt is made to allocate common overhead, nor is there concern that each segment should carry its "fair share of

[3] See James S. Earley, "Recent Developments in Cost Accounting and the 'Marginal Analysis,' " *Journal of Political Economy*, LXIII (June, 1955), 227-42.

11

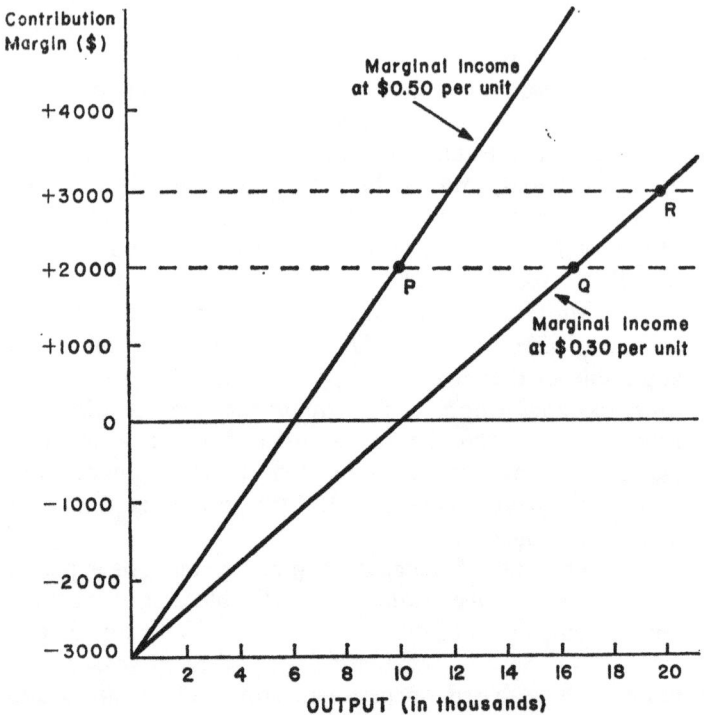

Figure 2. A segment profit chart prepared according to marginal income analysis concepts

For an example of one use of this management accounting tool, assume that the segment has escapable fixed costs of $3,000, variable costs of $0.50 per unit, sales price of $1.00 per unit, and output at 10,000 units (P). The contribution of this segment is then $2,000, as read from the vertical axis. Management proposes to lower the price to $0.80 in an effort to stimulate volume in this segment. The extent to which this decision is profitable depends upon the responsiveness of demand to price decreases. For example, an increase in output from 10,000 units to 17,000 (Q) results in the same contribution margin ($2,000), but if output increases to 20,000 units (R), contribution margin will increase to $3,000. Thus, an estimate of elasticity of demand must accompany the estimate of cost variability for the analysis to be complete.

overhead." Rather, the relevant criterion is measured in terms of the ratio of marginal balance (contribution) to investment employed in each segment.

3. *Merchandise management accounting (M.M.A.)* is an application of programed analysis to retail stores.[4] M.M.A. is one of several recent developments in retailing which attempt to focus attention on the proper use of variable cost information. In particular, attention is directed away from gross margins in merchandising decisions to controllable profits which reflect variable costs of items. This is consistent with the intent of previously discussed programed analyses.

M.M.A. illustrates the growing concern for incremental information in retailing. A similar development, contribution plan accounting, is also replacing methods emphasizing gross markups and net income. Contribution plan accounting places emphasis on the contribution of departments to indirect costs (all of which may not be fixed); M.M.A. goes one step further by emphasizing the contribution of each inventory item to fixed costs.

Limitations of programed analyses. This short discussion of programed analyses merely introduces the principles underlying these methods; it also raises several objections.

There are accounting techniques designed to systematize the flow of data for operating decisions. Yet these methods serve multiple purposes and may not always supply the data needed for a particular decision.

These programed analyses make use of many simplifying assumptions in separating fixed and variable elements of costs. Once established in the accounts, the separation may be used in decisions for which the original assumptions are not valid.

[4] See Robert I. Jones, *Merchandise Management Accounting in Practice* (Chicago: Arthur Anderson and Co., 1957); special issue on merchandise management accounting, *Journal of Retailing,* XXXIV (Spring, 1958); Malcolm P. McNair and Eleanor G. May, "Pricing for Profit: A Revolutionary Approach to Retail Accounting," *Harvard Business Review,* XXXV (May-June, 1957), 105-22.

There is, therefore, the question of whether any such routinized separation of costs might encourage inflexibility and lead to unsound business decisions.

Nonprogramed analyses. Ad hoc analyses attempt to overcome the alleged weaknesses of systematic accumulation of data. A leading spokesman for specific cost analysis, William Vatter, contends that the weaknesses of programed analyses are too great to overcome: each decision is concerned with a unique situation which requires special data.[5]

Special cost analysis based on income statements is one approach to nonprogramed analysis. Projected statements can be prepared for each alternative course of action. The alternative which has the greatest income potential is favored, subject to certain qualifications. For example, the increased income may be less than what management considers an adequate return on additional investment. Projecting the entire income statement is not necessary; it is possible to restrict attention to the costs and revenues that will change as a result of the decision.

Nonprogramed analyses do overcome the one important weakness of programed methods: the accounting data for each decision are selected especially for the situation. But, no matter how carefully selected, accounting data cannot cover all the important costs. With the application of the correct principles of decision making, the manager of the small firm can take the relevant information from his accounts while bearing in mind its limitations.

MANAGERIAL ECONOMICS IN BUSINESS DECISIONS

Economics has both descriptive and prescriptive sides. As a descriptive science, it attempts to generalize about the relations among economic variables; this requires the study of

[5] "Tailor-Making Cost Data for Specific Uses," *N.A.C.A. Bulletin, 1954 Conference Proceedings*, pp. 1691-1707. Reprinted in William E. Thomas, Jr. (ed.), *Readings in Cost Accounting, Budgeting and Control* (Cincinnati: South-Western Publishing Co., 1955), pp. 314-32.

actual behavior. But, as prescription, economics often proceeds in a nonempirical way, starting with certain premises and deriving logical consequences. Much of managerial economics follows the latter course. It often starts, for example, with the simplifying assumption that the firm seeks to maximize profits; the analysis then develops the logical conclusions following from that assumption. This is not the end of managerial economics, however, for there may be cases in which the assumption of profit maximization is not appropriate and adjustments for other objectives are necessary. It may turn out that the conclusions derived from strict logic are difficult or expensive to apply in actual business, so that modifications to meet the actualities of business are necessary. At the outset, managerial economics frequently assumes that information is cost free, so that the manager can inject the necessary data into a logical model and simply await the results. In actual practice the cost of data collection may preclude the use of the most refined analysis.

The principles of managerial economics

The logic of managerial economics is simple when examined in broad perspective. When applied to business problems, it may be contained in four basic principles.

1. The Incremental Principle: *a decision is sound if it increases revenue more than costs, or if it reduces costs more than revenue.*

A decision involves change, often in both costs and revenues. The incremental principle simply states that it is necessary to compare incremental costs with incremental revenues. This means that average costs, or full costs, and average revenues are not the proper focus of attention. Our case studies show, however, that many decisions are, in fact, based on average or full costs and that this practice is not always in conflict with the incremental principle.

Unfortunately, the concepts of incremental cost and incremental revenue are ambiguous and vary according to the time perspective. A cost which is not incremental for a short period may be incremental in the long run. Furthermore the distinction between the short run and the long run is not nearly so neat in business practice as in the elementary economics textbook. As we show, some decisions involving a few months of time will be similar in character to decisions in other industries involving many years. There is a whole range of short runs, depending on the nature of the issue at hand. Some decisions require only a consideration of immediate effects; others involve estimation of the total consequences of the decision over a period of time.

2. The Principle of Time Perspective: *a decision should take into account the shortrun and the longrun effects on revenue and costs, giving appropriate weight to the most relevant time periods.*

Perhaps a few simple illustrations will reduce the ambiguities of this principle. Take, for example, a decision whether or not to accept a particular order for which the customer has specified that he will pay no more than $5.00 per unit for 1,000 units. Suppose that the full cost is $7.00, but that the incremental cost is $4.00. This difference arises from the fact that certain costs included in full costs are unaffected by the decision—they will run on whether or not the order is taken. Considered on a shortrun basis, the incremental revenue of $5,000 and the incremental cost of $4,000 produce $1,000 of added income. It is necessary, however, to examine possible longer run repercussions. Will this customer and others refuse to pay higher prices in the future if a price concession is made now? Will prices paid by other customers be affected? Will the offer tie up productive capacity which might be used for more lucrative orders?

A similar study of both longrun and shortrun considerations enters into the decision on raising prices when demand is favorable. This point is discussed more fully in connection with individual cases.

3. The Discounting Principle: *if a decision affects costs and revenues at future dates, it is necessary to discount those*

16

costs and revenues down to present values before a valid comparison of alternatives is possible.

The discounting principle is particularly important in the evaluation of investment decisions, especially on fixed assets expected to last for a long time. There may be cases, especially when only a short period is involved, in which discounting can be ignored for practical purposes, but such cases are better examined individually.

Discounting reflects the fact that revenues far in the future have less value today than those nearer at hand. A dollar to be earned ten years from now is less valuable than one tomorrow, for there will be no opportunity to earn revenue from it in the ten-year period. To illustrate, $38.54 in cash today will at cumulative earnings of 10 percent amount to $100 ten years from now. If 10 percent is the true earning rate (opportunity cost of capital), then $100 to be earned ten years from now is worth no more than $38.54. We discount the $100 by dividing it by $(1+r)^n$ (where r is the interest rate and n the number of years) to determine its present value. In this case the failure to discount means that we overvalue future dollars by almost three times as compared with present dollars.

4. The Opportunity Cost Principle: *decision making requires a careful measurement of opportunity costs, that is, of the sacrifices required by a decision.*

The discounting principle is closely related to a broader concept, of which it is actually a particular application—the concept of opportunity costs. The cost of selecting any alternative in making a decision consists of the sacrifice of other alternatives required by that decision. One of the costs of taking a vacation trip, for example, is the sacrifice of the gardening one might have accomplished. Since a cost is a cost only if a sacrifice is involved, we can state dogmatically that all costs relevant to decision making are opportunity costs.

The incremental costs discussed earlier in this chapter are opportunity costs. The reason that fixed or sunk costs are irrelevant to some decisions is that the decision will not affect them—no sacrifice is required. It is not reasonable to let a decision be influenced by so-called "costs" which, in fact, involve no pain of any kind and no impact on profits.

A variety of cost concepts

Perhaps this is the appropriate point to introduce certain cost concepts that will appear at various points in this study, with some clarification of how they are related. "Marginal cost" is a widely used term in economics closely related to the "incremental cost" concept already mentioned. By marginal cost is meant the increase in total cost resulting from adding one more unit of output. By incremental cost is meant the change in total cost resulting from a decision. While the two terms are often used to mean the same thing, the latter is more flexible, since it can be applied not only to volume changes but to any other changes in costs resulting from a decision. Also incremental costs are not necessarily (or usually) restricted to a change in one unit of volume. Since businessmen usually think in terms of finite changes in volume, the incremental cost concept is probably more suited to our purposes than the marginal cost concept. In any case, both the incremental and marginal cost concepts are an application of what is known as "marginalism" in economics—the comparison of changes in totals.

The distinction between fixed and variable costs is too well known to require much discussion here. Usually this distinction refers to shortrun volume-cost relationships, the fixed costs being those unaffected by volume of output and the variable costs being those affected by volume. But in decision making, volume may not always be the issue; we may speak, therefore, of the fixed costs as those that are not affected by the decision and of the variable costs as those that are affected. Variable costs may run close to the marginal or incremental costs, and often it is convenient to use them synonomously.

The distinction between "implicit costs" and "explicit

costs" will be important in some of the case discussions. Explicit costs are those recognized in the accounting statements. But these statements do not always take into account all of the costs of interest to the economist; in other words, they do not reflect all of the opportunity costs. "Implicit costs" are opportunity costs not explicitly recognized in the accounting statements. The most elementary illustration is the wage of the owner in a sole proprietorship, that is, the income he has sacrificed by not working for someone else. Very commonly income statements do not take into account the implicit cost involved in the fact that the stockholder's funds are tied up in the firm rather than invested in other income-producing opportunities. This cost is often referred to as "implicit interest."

The expression "sunk costs" is the antithesis of incremental costs. They are totally unaffected by any decisions that might be made. In practical decision-making problems some costs are not sunk, but are nevertheless fixed as far as the specific shortrun decision is concerned. In fact, just what is "fixed" and what is "incremental" varies from one problem to the next. Another useful expression is "escapable costs," which is really a variation of "incremental costs," but which brings out forcefully that the decision involves a reduction in cost rather than an increase. For example, if the issue is one of abandoning a product line, it is extremely important to determine which costs will be avoided by the decision and which will continue.

Another widely known distinction—one that is common in accounting practice—is that between direct and overhead costs (burden). Direct costs are those that can be attributed directly to a particular product or department. The overhead costs are common costs, such as administrative costs or general plant costs that cannot be allocated except on some arbitrary basis. The expression "direct costs" is sometimes used in the same sense as variable costs—thus relating to cost-volume relationships rather than to the ease with which they may be attributed to particular operations.

19

Economists' criticism of traditional accounting

Managerial economics provides one framework of thought against which we can evaluate the relevance of accounting to decision making. Writers on the subject have noted a number of limitations of traditional accounting practices when examined in the light of economic theory.[6] We shall discuss the limitations most pertinent to this study.

(1) *The orientation of accounting to the past rather than to the future.* The primary task of accounting is the recording of historical events, as opposed to the estimating of future, uncertain events. There is a strong tradition that accounting should reflect actual incurred costs. The accounting profession and regulatory agencies have attempted to limit the amount of personal judgment by establishing "conventions," "principles," or "standards." These "guides to action" govern the manner in which data are treated in the accounts.[7]

The managerial economist is less interested than the accountant, however, in such historical costs and events. He is concerned with future revenues and costs, and the impact of decisions on these costs. To the economist, it is irrational to permit past costs to influence movements toward optimum positions in the future. What he needs is the knowledge of how a decision will affect future flows of funds into and out of the firm. The economist points to specific cases in which the emphasis on historical data has distorted the decision-making process. We shall be looking for illustrations of this distortion in the studies of small business cases that follow.

(2) *The arbitrary allocation of overhead costs.* Cost

---

[6] Joel Dean, *Managerial Economics* (Englewood Cliffs, N. J.: Prentice-Hall, 1951), pp. 12-28.

[7] These remarks refer to the traditional core of accounting. Accounting can be defined broadly to permit estimates, judgments, predictions, and the other features required by managerial economics. For a broad definition of accounting, see "Report of the Committee on Management Accounting," *Accounting Review*, XXXV (July, 1960), 400.

accountants usually make it a practice to allocate overhead costs to cost centers and to individual products. It is unnecessary to review the bases of these allocations; specific illustrations will appear later. The economist raises several questions about allocation procedures. To the extent that the overhead costs are fixed costs, the economist argues that they are irrelevant to business decisions, so that no allocation is necessary. In any case he doubts that routine systems of allocation are invariably appropriate to the variety of decisions.

(3) *The failure to reflect the true opportunity cost.* The accountant's historical costs reflect the opportunity costs only by coincidence. Often the accountant understates costs, for his measurements do not reflect certain sacrifices involved in choice. "Implicit interest" and "imputed wages" are two of many illustrations. The accountant hesitates to record a cost unless there is an asset outlay. This means that he will fail to record the full opportunity cost of using a building whose value for alternative purposes may be much greater than the expenses recorded on the books. He may not charge as a cost of expanding one product the sacrifices that may be required by the contraction of others.

(4) *The failure of the depreciation charge to reflect the true loss in economic value.* The economist is frequently dissatisfied with the depreciation expense figure computed by the accountant. Traditionally this figure is based on historical costs rather than future sacrifices; it may not reflect the expected loss in the value of assets that is relevant. The problem is not simply one of replacement cost versus historical cost as a basis for depreciation—a subject that has received a great deal of attention in accounting literature. More important, accounting data do not measure the future loss in value that may be required by a decision, for example, to retain a piece of equipment rather than to replace it.

(5) *The use of shortcuts to accumulate and present data.* A more general criticism—one that encompasses part of those already discussed—is that accounting takes a number

of shortcuts in the accumulation and presentation of information that fall short of the refinement required by a complete application of economic analysis. The common routine of accounting procedures that runs through financial accounting, cost accounting, and even some of the variable costing techniques fails to measure the exact quantities needed for each decision. Even in special studies, the accountant tends to take shortcuts, as is illustrated by the "accountant's method" for handling investment decisions.

The fact that accounting does not do everything that economic theory might ask of it is not necessarily a criticism of accounting practices. Since traditional accounting and economics are concerned with different questions, it should be no surprise that they often find different answers. There can be no dogmatic conclusions about what degree of theoretical refinement is justified in practical, day-to-day business, especially the small business in which the expenses of refinement are a real barrier to the full application of economic analysis. We hope that an intensive study of actual cases will help determine the extent to which small firms can afford to carry their analysis, whether this analysis is accounting or economic in character.

2

GARDEN AND LANDSCAPE NURSERIES

*A*T FIRST glance one might well wonder at the significance attached to plant nurseries by giving over a whole chapter to discussing them. But in the nursery industry the contribution of accounting to decisions is of such special interest that it deserves a full discussion. In some respects nurseries stand in an extreme position—one at which the usual accounting methods appear to offer the least to decision making. The question is whether a development of new accounting methods or of new tools for the systematic application of economic analysis is warranted in the nursery industry.

This chapter covers only nurseries that grow a majority of their own plants. It is not concerned with retail nurseries that purchase their plants; their problems are much like those of the retailers discussed later. Three types of nurseries are covered: (1) two retail nurseries, which engage in the wholesale business on a small scale both as buyers and sellers, but concentrate on propagating and growing plants for sale directly to the consumer; (2) two wholesale nurseries, which sell most of their product to retail outlets of various sorts—garden stores, landscaping firms, etc., and also do a small volume of direct retail business; (3) one landscaping firm, which grows plants only because the management believes there is no other dependable source of supply.

The first part of this chapter is empirical, summarizing findings on the actual practices of these nurseries. The second and main part, however, involves the construction of a theoretical economic model against which actual practice is evaluated.

Interviews with the managers of these nurseries suggest that the following decisions are among the most important.

1. What plants to propagate and grow. These decisions govern the allocation of the nursery's land to various plant materials. We can call these "plant mix" decisions.

2. What prices to charge for the coming season.

3. What prices to reduce and what plants to destroy when plants tie up land longer than is economical.

4. At what ages plants are to be sold. These decisions are closely related to the pricing decisions, but there are times at which a nursery may discourage or refuse a sale at the quoted price in order to permit a plant to mature.

This list of crucial decisions is arbitrary. Other decisions may be of equal importance—such as those concerning advertising and sales promotion or those concerning the hiring of personnel.[1] Rather than cover the whole range of de-

[1] As a matter of fact one owner-manager clearly was more concerned with his personnel situation than with other problems—and for good reasons.

cisions, we confine the discussion to those listed, especially the first two.

SOME GENERALIZATIONS

While the sample of firms is small and not altogether representative, we believe that several generalizations on the role of accounting in nurseries can be justified. These are based not only on the case interviews, but also on discussions with industry authorities, and on articles in bulletins and trade journals.

1. Accounting plays an insignificant role in the crucial decisions in the nursery business. Cost accounting is almost unknown, but there have been experiments with cost finding; most nursery people apparently do not believe these experiments have been profitable. Little attempt is made to determine the costs of particular product lines. In fact, even the separation of the costs of landscaping from those of retailing and those of propagation and growing is usually done loosely and inaccurately. One of the firms studied does break revenue data down into 21 categories but has been less successful in allocating costs to these categories.

2. When accounting does influence nursery decision making, it is through the income statement. The concept of homeostasis introduced in Chapter 1 seems to describe the way some of the nursery managers make use of accounting information. If their annual income seems "unreasonably" low—that is, if it falls short of some predetermined standard of appropriate income—the managers become interested in action that will correct the situation. They may then go over their price lists for the coming year and raise prices on items they "feel" are not making the requisite profit. Since they have no cost figures on individual plants, they do not really know which items are unprofitable, but they have subjective beliefs (supported by knowledge of the relative labor time expended on different products, etc.). Their ability to raise prices is conditioned

by market demand; they are unable to raise prices on some unprofitable lines.

Similarly, dissatisfaction with profits may lead to reconsideration of the plant mix, with a gradual shift to plants that are thought to be more profitable. But our case studies suggest that propagation and growing decisions are more frequently affected by the volume of sales than by estimates of profits; if a plant is "moving," the nursery continues to grow it. If the trend of volume of certain items is upward, the nursery usually allocates more space to them.

While the one accounting figure that does seem to influence decision making is "income," this figure is rather peculiar because of the nature of accounting in the nursery industry.[2] The nurseries covered in this study measure their income without regard to the inventory of plants. Some of them operate on a "cash" basis. But even the firm that maintains accounts on an accrual basis does not estimate the value of plants; this is done in conformity with income tax regulations. Thus a nursery that ends a year with a greater volume of plant materials in the ground or in the warehouse than at the beginning does not reflect this fact in its income figure. From a practical point of view there is much to be said for not taking the increased value of inventory into account, for any estimates of such values are inevitably conjectural. From the economic point of view, however, it does not make sense to ignore inventories, for they represent values as much as other assets. Therefore the accounting figure that has the greatest influence on decisions in nurseries is somewhat questionable.

3. All the firms covered by this study are concerned with demand and the competition underlying demand in their decisions. Some of the managers stress cost considera-

[2] It is possible that even this phase of accounting is not of great importance in decision making. When nurserymen talk about "income," they probably are not always referring to a figure on the income statement. In small firms there is usually some knowledge of income before the accountant makes up his statements.

tions at the beginning of the interviews, but all of them give examples of how demand factors tend to dominate some decisions. Demand as used here includes the forces of competition, that is, the prices charged by other nurseries and the likelihood that other nurseries might react to the policies of the firm under study. Several specific illustrations from the case studies should clarify this point.

One manager stated that he could not charge more for his flowering shrubs (even though they were not "profitable") because he had to face the competition of plants grown more cheaply in a favorable climate elsewhere. He continued to grow the plants because some customers expected him to maintain a complete line. He recognized that competition placed a ceiling on what he could charge.

Another manager discussed the same point in a different way. He felt the pressure of competition from nurseries to the south and north: to the south, cost and prices are lower; to the north, they are higher. He thought that he had to maintain his prices between these two. But it became clear upon further questioning that he did not study the prices of these competing nurseries systematically. He "believed" that he set his prices between the two levels.

Most of the firms used rather informal forecasting procedures for estimating future demand. These forecasts were the basis for planting decisions, which would, of course, determine what plants would be available in future years. One procedure was to note trends—for example, the movement to ranch style houses, for which tall evergreens are not suited—and to project these trends into the future. Another was to discuss developments with customers (especially in the case of the wholesale growers whose customers were retailers closer to the ultimate market). One manager consulted builders about new developments in housing and their implications for the demand for plants.

Why cost accounting is not used

Why do nursery managers not make greater use of cost

27

accounting? The interviewees suggested a number of reasons.

1. The erratic behavior of the weather and its unpredictable effects on different kinds of plants make it difficult to estimate costs. Should one take into account in measuring the costs of a particular plant the fact that the past winter was particularly severe and wiped out half of the crop, or should one try to average such losses over the years?

2. It is difficult to allocate labor costs to the various plants or even to the major categories of business. All the firms transfer workers constantly from one activity to another; hence it is difficult to determine how much time is spent on each. One of the firms goes to a great deal of trouble to keep time records on various categories of business, but the management complains that the employees do not make accurate entries.

3. A difficult conceptual problem of allocating the costs of the land occurs, especially when land values are changing rapidly, as is true for those nurseries located near cities. Similarly, the allocation of other overhead costs, such as management time, presents problems.

4. The problem of how to treat the costs of destroyed materials is difficult to solve. Nurseries find it necessary to destroy plants that are using up valuable space but have not been sold. As such plants get older and larger, the costs of removing them rises and the amount of land a single plant ties up increases.[3] Therefore a time comes when plants must be destroyed. It is difficult to determine in advance the cost of destruction and how it should be allocated.

Though these reasons for the failure to make use of cost accounting are representative, there may be others equally important or perhaps even more fundamental. The buildup of costs by adding together labor, materials, and overhead, which is common in manufacturing, does not

[3] This results from the fact that as more and more plants are sold from a given block of land, the remaining plants occupy more land per unit.

seem applicable to decision making in the nursery business. Knowing the "full cost" of each item is not particularly important, though it is desirable to have information about incremental costs. The allocation of the rentals on land is likewise unnecessary, even misleading, and the same is true for the allocation of overhead. Too much effort on normal cost accounting procedures could do more harm than good by distracting management's attention from the factors that should influence key decisions.

In some cases cost analysis may be profitable. One of the firms made a special study of its truck costs, finding that in some seasons the use of three-man crews on trucks was uneconomical. The study led to the reduction of the crews to two men in July, August, September, January, and February. The same firm made a thorough study of the proportion of time its trucks were in use and determined that it would be economical to purchase an extra truck as a standby. No doubt such analyses are useful, but they are quite different from determinations of how much different plants "cost."

Very strangely, few of the managers interviewed had given formal attention to one of their most important costs from the economic point of view—the opportunity cost in growing one variety rather than alternatives.[4] If one wanted to measure the cost of a particular variety of plants, he should be concerned as to whether that variety takes three years or ten years to mature, since the longer period involves a greater cumulative sacrifice of revenue from alternatives. Doubtless the prices these nurseries charge do reflect the time periods required in maturing plants (prices for large plants are almost universally higher than those for small ones of the same variety). The managers recognize that land is tied up longer on such plants, but they do not appear to have thought through the discounting principles involved in a sound treatment of this problem.

[4] For a full discussion of the opportunity cost concept, see Chapter 2.

A note on nursery cost accounting literature

Articles on nursery accounting confirm the conclusion that cost accounting has not made much progress in the industry.[5] Most of the systems that have been tried are not the usual cost systems. Some consist of piecemeal attempts at controlling certain costs, for example, by establishing standard labor times; others may be described as "cost finding"—*ad hoc* methods of determining the full cost of certain operations. Some systems merely try to allocate revenues and costs to different activities in the hope that this will show the relative profitability of these activities.

Most of the nurseries' cost accounting appears to be directed at the costs of landscaping. The objective here is to obtain estimates of the times required for various landscaping jobs (including travel time), to serve as the basis for pricing. The nursery accounting literature has a "full cost" bias and shows very little evidence of any impact of economic analysis.

A PRESCRIPTIVE MODEL FOR NURSERIES

Few nurseries apply any formal analysis to decision making. The question is whether an economic model for rational decision making would be profitable in the industry. The construction of such a model should in any case help evaluate present methods used by management in reaching decisions and should also provide an additional basis for analyzing the role of accounting.

An economic model for the nursery industry starts with "revenue estimating" rather than "cost accounting." The initial construction of the model involves drastic simplifying assumptions, most of which are removed as the discussion proceeds, drawing the analysis to a closer approximation of reality. The initial assumptions are:

[5] See W. J. Billerbeck, "Cost Accounting for the Nurseryman," *American Nurseryman*, CX (Nov. 1, 1959), 14, 60-71. Also Harold Hunziker, *Knowing Your Landscape Costs* (Davenport, Iowa: National Landscape Nurserymen's Association, 1957).

1. The nursery owns a given amount of land.

2. The demand schedules for all the plants are known with certainty. This means not only that the immediate demand is known; it also means that the position of demand at future dates within the decision-making "horizon" is known.

3. The breakdown between fixed and variable costs is known.

4. The risks due to weather, plant disease, etc., are known.

5. There are no difficulties in allocating incremental costs to particular plants.

6. The cost of capital is known.

7. The firm wishes to maximize profits.

Certainty model: plant mix decisions

Suppose the nursery owns land that is completely clear of plants and wishes to make decisions about the plant mix. Under the given assumptions management can make rational planting decisions simply by applying economic analysis. The problem is to select those plants in quantities that maximize the future net revenues (revenues minus incremental costs) from the land. The objective is to maximize the contribution that future net revenues make to fixed costs and profits.

It is clear that a correct evaluation of future revenues and costs must involve application of the discounting principle. Revenues expected from plants sold five years hence should be discounted more heavily than revenues to be received two years from now. The longer the time before harvest, the longer the resources of the company are tied up and the greater the sacrifice of revenues from alternative activities that are involved. The cost of capital, which is assumed to be known, should be used as the discount rate.[6]

---

[6] The determination of the cost of capital is a highly technical subject beyond the scope of this volume. It requires that the manager make estimates of rates of return that can be earned in alternative investments. In view of confusion on the subject, it seems fair to say that the subjective estimates of management should suffice.

There are two theoretically correct formulas for handling the discounting problem: computation of the *discounted rate of return* (which can be compared with the cost of capital) and estimation of the *present value* (which requires discounting of future revenues and costs by the cost of capital). These formulas may be found in any book on capital budgeting or managerial economics. The present discussion uses the present value approach. The rule for rational decision making is to *maximize the discounted contribution that future net revenues make to fixed costs and profits,* which means maximization of present value.

The application of the model described so far involves several complications, some of which are peculiar to nurseries and similar industries.

1. The flow of future revenues is uneven in nurseries; there are no revenues at the beginning. This is unlike the usual investment situation in manufacturing in which revenues or savings appear almost as soon as the equipment is installed.

2. The estimates of revenues must take into account the complementarity of demand for nursery products. The offering of one plant may help "fill out" the product line and help sell other plants. This means that the present value of a plant may be greater than that indicated by its own sales. This problem of complementarity is found also in other industries, especially in retailing.

3. Decisions on the quantity of land to be devoted to a particular plant must recognize price-volume relationships. If it requires lower prices to sell greater quantities of a plant material, it becomes necessary to consider the marginal revenues rather than the average or total revenues. The price-volume relationship or elasticity of demand in turn depends upon the market structure in which the nursery operates.

One great advantage of the present value method is that it provides a ready comparison of plants of varying growing periods. To make two plants requiring different growing periods comparable, it is necessary to estimate the present value of revenues and costs for the same length of time in the future on each. Here the "horizon" or planning period concept becomes important. As used in this chapter, the term "horizon," or "planning period," refers to the maximum growing period that a nursery considers on the slowest maturing plant. The model requires a projection of revenues and expenses on all varieties up to the full length of the "horizon." If the "horizon" is nine years, it is necessary to consider three cycles of a plant with a three-year growing period to make an adequate comparison.

Certainty model: pricing decisions

Under the assumed conditions, the rules for pricing are clear cut though complicated. It should be noted at the outset that plant mix decisions are dependent upon the pricing decisions—that is, it is necessary to determine the most profitable price simultaneously with the most profitable mix of plants. The determination of the "best" price involves marginal principles well known in economics. A high price may mean low volume and thus does not guarantee the maximum contribution to overhead and profits. A low price may mean low contribution per unit that is not offset by a large volume. The elasticity of demand helps govern the determination of the best price.

The difficulty here is the determination of the "best" price on one item independently from prices on others. It may be that the contribution to overhead and profits from growing ten acres of a particular type of tree selling at a price of $5.00 is greater than that from five acres at $6.00 or fifteen acres at $4.00, but this does not mean that ten acres of this plant should be grown. What is necessary is a computation of the discounted *marginal* contribution per unit of land. The aim should be to equate the discounted *marginal* contributions from each plant variety—that is, to expand the production and lower the price on high contribution items and contract the production and raise the price on low contribution items until both make the same discounted marginal contribution per unit of land.

Certainty model: other decisions

Take, for example, a problem that is quite common in nurseries. Five evergreens are left on a particular block of land.[7] If they were cleared from the land, the whole block could be planted anew. Three alternatives are available.

1. Let the five evergreens grow until the next season in the hope that they will be sold at that time.

2. Sell the evergreens at a reduced price and plant the land in the new crop.

3. Clear the evergreens from the land, making way for the new crop.[8]

The solution would involve a comparison of three values: (1) the discounted contribution to overhead and profits of the five evergreens sold in the next season; (2) the revenue to be derived from a cut-price sale at the present (taking into account the effects of this price reduction on company sales in general) plus the discounted extra revenue to be gained from an earlier planting of the new item; and (3) the discounted extra revenue from an earlier planting of the new item less the incremental costs of plant destruction.

This illustration indicates the flexibility of the analysis suggested so far. The main issue before us is whether it is or could be feasible in practice.

Cost considerations

One of the main points made so far is that decision making in nurseries should concentrate on revenue estimation rather than cost measurement. But costs are not com-

[7] Under the conditions of certainty with which we started, this eventuality would not arise. But it is time to start relaxing the assumptions.

[8] A nursery may select the third alternative rather than the second because of the chances that lower prices on some units will "spoil the market" on others or because of the cost and nuisance of special sales.

pletely irrelevant.[9] Since we are interested in determining the *contribution* of revenues to the land and other fixed facilities of the firm, it is unnecessary to deduct any of the fixed or "sunk" costs from those revenues. But it is necessary to take into account the *incremental costs.*

One may define incremental costs several different ways in this situation—and indeed some flexibility in definition may help meet the needs of different decision-making problems. We are interested in those costs which arise from growing one plant rather than another. What would enter into such costs? Some nurserymen might be tempted to include all of the labor costs; but a substantial proportion of the labor costs will run on regardless of the mix of plants. The emphasis should be on the *differences* in labor costs arising from different plantings. The same would be true of the costs of fertilizer, sprays, extra advertising, or whatever added costs arise from the particular decision.

In actual practice, difficulties may arise in estimating such incremental costs precisely. But there is every reason to believe that such estimates are easier and more relevant than estimates of fully allocated average costs, which depend upon arbitrary allocations of fixed costs. It is not necessary, for example, to estimate the cost of land—which is fortunate, since that would raise questions about whether it is "original cost," "replacement cost," or "market value" that is relevant.

Significance of the present value approach

What the present value approach to decision making means is this: the emphasis is on the apportionment of the fixed facilities (the land, the buildings, the services of top management, the fixed component of the labor force, and

[9] This discussion assumes that most nursery costs are fixed, so that only a minor fraction of the costs appears in the incremental costs. This is consistent with our observations in the nurseries we have visited. If incremental costs are a high proportion of the total, the relative stress we have given revenue would no longer be appropriate, especially in view of the fact that the costs come earlier and thus should not be discounted so heavily.

the equipment) to various products. The objective is maximization of profits to be derived from those facilities, which means the selection of the optimum combination of alternatives. (If the objective is *not* maximization of profits, some modification of the model would be necessary.) The present value method discounts the expected profits in such a way that earnings in different time periods can be compared.

The fixed facilities, including the land, are the scarce resources that must be rationed according to this model. The present values enable management to rank alternatives to optimize the use of these resources. This is not necessarily the only way to look at the problem. If the firm is in a tight cash position, management might look upon liquid funds rather than land as the bottleneck resource and might place greater stress on the early receipt of cash from sales, thus giving a higher priority to short-maturing plants. But the present value model can handle this problem. What a shortage of cash really means is that the opportunity cost of capital is high.[10] The higher the rate of discount, the more favorable the investments in early maturing plants according to the formula, for it discounts revenues from slow-growing plants more heavily.

Removal of the simplifying assumptions

Practical nurserymen are probably highly skeptical of the practicability of the model. It is remote from their experience, and the estimates and computations required go far beyond what most of them believe they can afford. One of the benefits of constructing such a model is that it brings out the difficulties of actual applications of theoretically correct methods and thus indicates the need for some kind of compromise.

The next step is to remove the most unrealistic assumptions, to bring the model closer to reality.

1. We remove the assumption of a given quantity of

[10] This is a reflection of the fact that the tight cash position restricts plantings to items producing high returns.

land. The model itself indicates when land should be purchased or sold. If the *present value* of *marginal* land in internal uses exceeds the price of added land, expansion is profitable.[11] If such *present values* are below the market value of the land, this suggests a contraction or perhaps a relocation on cheaper land. Thus the present value method aids longrun decisions.

2. We drop the assumption of certainty about demand, revenues, and costs. The firms face several kinds of uncertainty, among which the following are most important: uncertainty about the position and the elasticity of the demand curves of the various products that the nursery might sell at various points in the future; uncertainty about the complementary relations among the demand schedules for these products (that is, uncertainty about cross elasticities); uncertainty about the effects of the weather and disease on the different lines of plants in the future; uncertainty about the relative proportions of fixed and variable costs, indeed about the shape of the cost functions over time; and uncertainty about the proportion of plant materials that remain unsold after a period of years, resulting in uncertainty about the costs of clearing the land for new planting.[12]

Probability analysis may be applied to all of these types of uncertainty. On the basis of past experience and future forecasts, management can make estimates of the dimensions of the probability distributions of demands and costs. It is then possible to apply the present value formula, the analysis being complicated by the fact that the estimates are probability distributions rather than exact estimates of costs and revenues.

The computation of these probabilities is likely to be

[11] For this purpose it may be desirable to lengthen the "horizon" to include a longer period of years. Otherwise the present value is understated.

[12] In other industries the present value of an investment frequently includes the discounted "salvage value" of the equipment at the end of its life. In nurseries the salvage value is frequently negative—it costs money to destroy the plants that remain in the ground.

laborious and costly. Even in theory there may be doubt that probability analysis is applicable. If the future is unlike any prospects that this firm or any other firm in the past has ever met, where does one get the information to determine the shapes and positions of the probability distributions? One may doubt that even a large nursery with a great volume of sales of each plant material could profit much from refined statistical analysis; and the smaller the nursery, the more doubtful the practice. Thus we have encountered a serious obstacle to the application of the model to the realities of business life.

CONCLUSIONS: ECONOMICS AND ACCOUNTING IN NURSERY DECISIONS

This chapter has considered two approaches to decision making: an accounting approach which follows the tradition of building up costs including allocations of overhead; and the approach of economics, which starts with revenue estimates, makes adjustments for incremental costs, and applies the discounting principle. A study of actual cases and of the literature indicates that neither approach has won wide popularity in the industry.

The simplicity of the accounting approach explains why some firms and writers have taken an interest in developing cost finding or cost accounting for nurseries. But we have shown that both conceptual and practical difficulties stand in the way of this development. Perhaps cost accounting can contribute to control; but measures of full cost have little to contribute to decision making.

The economic model we have constructed also has serious limitations. If applied formally, it takes on a mathematical form, since it requires the simultaneous consideration of a large number of variables. Its full application might require an electronic computer. The variables fitted into this model must be subjective estimates of future events, including forecasts of demand. Even the determination of the appropriate discount rate requires something close to a guess. The economic model is a refined technique for dealing with highly conjectural data.

Is there anything practical a nurseryman can gain from this discussion? Perhaps the analysis in this chapter will give him greater confidence that his failure to use cost accounting is no great loss. He may learn from the economic model despite its complexity. It points up the factors that should influence decisions. In fact, many nurserymen untrained in economics are undoubtedly approximating the kind of analysis called for by this model.

A recent article for nurserymen supports the view presented here: "The best thing for them [nurserymen] to do is make some guesses on what can be sold, plant these selections, do the best possible job of production, do all possible to keep expenses down, and when the crop is ready, do all within reason to sell it at the highest possible price. . . . A nurseryman is far better qualified to set prices if he is thoroughly acquainted with the year's . . . production, market demands, carry-over, . . . general business conditions and similar contingencies that joggle demands up and down. In fact cost figures might have the effect of leading him to price his trees much below or much above what he should and thus he may realize far less than he would have without this cost knowledge."[13]

The theory presented in this chapter is useful in spite of the inadequacies of the data available in practice. A full recognition of the role of discounting, of the importance of demand and competition, and of the significance of incremental costs should lead to better decision making. Nurserymen will continue to make subjective estimates of these variables, but those familiar with the theory are more likely to make relevant estimates.

[13] Billerbeck, *Amer. Nurseryman,* CX, 62. This same writer favors special cost analyses and controls to serve particular purposes. For example, he samples time cards on certain operations and uses these for control. But apparently he is quite careful to avoid letting his cost estimates have an undue influence on his decisions.

3

RETAIL STORES

$\mathcal{I}$N CONDUCTING his business each retailer has problems that are unique to the operation of his own firm, and retailing deals with a diverse array of products, each requiring slightly different handling by management.[1] Yet there are kinds of decisions common to the whole area. Typical of important decisions for successful retailing are: determination of what and how much to buy; pricing; establishment or abandonment of merchandise lines; total promotional effort; and allocation of promotional effort. Questions of buying and pricing are probably the most fundamental decisions which the retailer must make, and therefore they form the center of this chapter.

SOME GENERALIZATIONS

Six general statements summarize the central findings from the case studies, but do not displace the fuller discussion of particular cases in the later part of this chapter.

1. The stores covered by this study accumulate accounting data primarily to satisfy governmental regulations and to maintain some semblance of financial control. Small stores do not emphasize decision making as a purpose of their accounting systems; larger stores sometimes make decisions on the basis of data secured for one of the two principal purposes.

2. The concept of homeostasis describes the usual role of accounting in retail decision making. This statement is made with some reservation because small retailers are in such close contact with their business that accounting reports merely confirm their impressions. The homeostatic function of accounting is more pronounced in large stores where decision-making authority is delegated.

3. Small retailers use sales data as a first approximation of future demand, though only in combination with other information. The final estimate of future demand is conditioned by the retailer's own judgment, employee suggestions, etc.

4. Budgeting is evident in some form in all firms. The extent to which the budget is formalized varies widely.

5. Accounting is not used by the stores covered in this study as a source of programed incremental cost data. When decisions require cost data, the merchants make *ad hoc* studies of anticipated costs.

6. Particular attention is given to suppliers' "estimated profitability" studies. This practice indicates that the store managements consider such studies relevant for merchandising decisions. It raises the question of why the same retailers do not make studies of their own.

[1] The case studies for this chapter cover men's clothing, gift, drug, book, hardware, department, and departmentalized specialty stores.

THE CONCEPT OF HOMEOSTASIS
AND RETAIL DECISION MAKING

Accounting can operate in the homeostasis process as (1) the receptor of changing conditions, (2) the translator of conditions into financial data, and (3) the relayer of data to the organization. But the extent to which these functions are performed depends upon the degree of refinement attained by the accounting system and the focus of management's attention.

Retailers stress the development of various financial and operating ratios. Trade associations by accumulating and publishing the operating results of retail stores encourage the practice. Store managers are in a position to compare their operating results with those of other stores; but, in order to use the information, managers must develop their own ratios. Two cases illustrate the wide variation in small retailer use of comparative data.

Edward's Men's Shop is located in a medium-size industrial city. The owner and one other salesman are the only personnel. The accounting system is very crude, and reports are prepared once a year for tax purposes. Ratios and averages are not prepared because the owner sees no need for them nor does he understand their meaning. He receives publications of industry data, but does not use the information.

In this case the concept of homeostasis may seem inapplicable because data are not developed to reveal changing relationships in the financial statements. However, the owner gauges his success by his ability to maintain an adequate living. If a cash stringency develops, his first reaction is to embark on a campaign which would ease the situation, e.g., drastic markdowns and increased advertising. The owner's demand for cash shifts over time. The Edwards case illustrates the homeostatic nature of decisions and indicates that accounting data are not necessary for the process to operate.

Gravett's is the largest men's clothing firm in a college city. This and several other stores contribute semiannual operating results to a central office which computes certain ratios and averages from the data. The contributing stores receive a report of the combined results. Store officials are stimulated to correct deficiencies revealed by the report.

This store maintains an elaborate accounting system (machine accounting makes possible perpetual inventory control), but there are no departmental reports even though the outlet is departmentalized for buying purposes. With machine accounting, day-by-day figures are available on sales and merchandise costs. The data are translated into average markups by related categories of items. The computation of these markups may raise doubts about management's statement that little attention is given to average markups.

Retailers are often more concerned with individual financial statement items than with relationships among items.

Martin's Men's Store was purchased in bankruptcy by a former employee of a national retail chain. The owner gave up a good salary to operate it. An extensive advertising campaign was undertaken to increase profits to a "satisfactory level." In three years, sales were doubled, and the owner was satisfied with profits. Subsequently, advertising expenditures were reduced because the objective was reached.

Profit is the concern of the owner, and in this case, profit is measured by accounting reports. Throughout the three years, operating statements were prepared biannually and the profit figure was consciously compared with the decision maker's profit objective.

The rationality of curtailing successful advertising is subject to question. But there are two possible interpretations: (1) the decision maker assumes that once the desired level of profit is reached, less advertising is necessary to maintain the captured market and the profit, or (2) he estimates that the advertising expense would exceed the incremental profits from advertising. Neither interpretation fits the actual situation: the owner having reached his goal cut back the advertising campaign without further thought. Throughout the three-year period, the owner regularly received reports of national data which, when compared with the firm's ratio of advertising to sales, showed the latter the higher. But to the owner this fact was secondary as long as profits were unsatisfactory. Once the profit goal was attained, advertising was budgeted at the national average.

To summarize, the stimuli for decision making vary from store to store. (1) In some stores formal accounting data do not appear in the homeostatic process. This is true in very small stores in which the accounting systems are quite crude. The owners are more concerned with cash than with "profit." (2) In larger stores, a great deal of time and effort is spent to compute and record ratios. The amount of effort is not always an indication of the importance of the data; in some cases, no uses of such information are cited, even though the statistics are available. (3) Although the homeostatic concept may suggest stress on ratios, the case studies indicate greater attention to absolutes. The firms are concerned with the amounts of cash, of salaries, or of profits.

HISTORICAL DATA AS
ESTIMATES OF FUTURE DATA

Historical data are used as first approximations of expectations, depending on the type of retailer. In the case studies, accounting data are frequently used in forecasts of demand. Merchandise decisions may rest on such estimates, but the final decision is influenced by a number of considerations which reduce the impact of accounting data.

Why historical data are used in some retail stores

Some stores use historical data in estimating future requirements, especially in the case of shopping goods with relatively stable demand. Such merchandise is usually handled by the smaller, more specialized retailer. For example, the small retailers of men's clothing state that data for the past are valid approximations of future sales. These retailers find that demand for their merchandise shifts very little over time.

Borons Men's Shop carries an exclusive line of merchandise, and patrons of the store are mainly from the high-income bracket. For seasonal merchandising decisions, previous season's sales data are consulted and orders are placed which differ little from those of the preceding season. It is significant that this retailer classifies sales by individual items, even though managements of stores with similar merchandise do not.

Using past data in decision making may appear to be inconsistent with managerial economics which emphasizes orientation to the future. The focus on past data is appropriate if there is a close relationship between past and future volume. Accounting systems can provide information on past sales and sales returns of individual or related merchandise. Other internal sources of information include customer and sales people suggestions. External sources of information for anticipating demand include buying office circulars, trade papers, newspapers, and market surveys.[2]

Accounting systems as sources of historical data

The accounting systems are rarely designed to develop relevant data explicitly for internal decision making. On the contrary, the systems exist to provide data for external parties (mainly government agencies) and for financial control. In only a few stores is management able to consult accounting records for information on the purchases and sales of individual items. Periodic inventory counts, usually taken preceding a buying trip or before placing an order, provide facts if the records disclose purchases of individual items.

Unger Men's Store keeps no records of purchases. When placing an order, the owner obtains information on previous purchases from the supplier.

[2] Delbert J. Duncan and Charles F. Phillips, *Retailing: Principles and Methods* (5th ed.; Homewood, Ill.: Richard D. Irwin, Inc., 1959), p. 248.

45

The manager of Unger's stated that more information relating to styles, colors, sizes, dates of sale, subsequent markdowns, etc., is desirable. But he does not collect such data. He regards the cost of doing so as prohibitive.

Another men's clothing store maintains simple, but complete, records on sales and purchases of individual items in its stock. The manager was quite emphatic in stating that his system was adequate for his needs and that his experience showed demand for the store's merchandise was stable.

To summarize: in some retail stores data regarding the past are a useful (but partial) indication of future demand; but the accounting systems in these stores do not usually develop the pertinent information systematically, if at all.

THE MERCHANDISE BUDGET

The merchandise budget is of concern only as it helps answer the question: what effect does budgeting have on merchandising decisions? The discussion throws light on three issues; (1) what the merchandise budget is; (2) how the budget is used in small firms; and (3) how it affects merchandising decisions.

The merchandise budget defined

Buying decisions consist of determining what to buy, how much to buy, when to buy, and from whom to buy. The merchandise budget does not resolve these issues, but it does provide a framework for planning purchases. Specifically, a merchandise budget is the formal, or informal, allocation of available funds among various competing inventory items. It is not a budget of costs and revenues; only wholesale costs are included in the merchandise budget. It may cover a three- to six-month period, or longer, depending upon the store's characteristics.

The budget and the small retailer

The allocations in the case studies are in terms of units, of dollars, or of both. When it is in terms of dollars (the predominant practice), the retailer attempts to maximize the gross margin on the sale of all items. Since price lines are usually firmly established in small retail stores, the emphasis is on "economic" buying. The objective is to buy merchandise of suitable quality to fit into the price range and at a wholesale cost which makes a satisfactory margin feasible. Unit budgeting is the rule in instances of prepriced, nationally advertised lines. In this situation, the retailer is concerned only with estimating the amount to sell at the established price.

Budgeting in small retail stores varies in several respects. In very small owner-manager firms, the process is very informal and subjective. For example, the owner determines the amount of available funds and then, from past records tempered by his own judgment, allocates funds among the various items. Other retailers buy as the occasion arises without preliminary planning.

In larger stores the process of budgeting is more formalized. If the buying function is delegated to other employees, the budgeting process is a means of controlling the expenditures of any single buyer. The Richardson case illustrates this point.

Richardson's Department Store is a successful operation in a large city. Although annual sales are in excess of $2 million, it is independently owned and is not dominant in the city. The merchandising manager allows each buyer to make up his buying plan (budget) for a coming season. Each buyer's budget is then compared with the master plan. If critical differences appear, the buyer and merchandising manager discuss the reasons and reach agreement. Once a plan is accepted, the buyer takes full responsibility for the operation of his department.

In this store, budgeting is a tool for administrative control—not merely for financial control. Smaller stores do not extend the budget beyond provision of a buying guide.

Its effect on merchandising decisions

It is difficult in small stores to distinguish budgeting

from the whole process of merchandising decisions. But one thing is clear: in those stores in which lines of merchandise are stable, the budgeting process is the merchandising decision. In such stores little effort is made to experiment with price or with new merchandise; the budget incorporates the expedient decision.

The budget can be a restraint on buying. It establishes the initial number (or value) of items to be purchased, but the retailer may leave a 10 percent to 30 percent "open to buy" margin in each category. During the season, reorders are made until the "open to buy" provision is nil. If merchandise is purchased beyond this limit, the retailer "overbuys." With certain exceptions, retailers do not reorder an item that is "100 percent bought."

The function of the budget, or merchandising plan, varies among stores. In a department store, the manager considers it an invaluable control device. In a small shop, the owner uses the budget to indicate where money is spent.

AD HOC ANALYSIS

Small retailers seldom prepare quantitative *ad hoc* analyses for merchandising decisions. The owner-managers of small shoe shops, men's clothing stores, etc., consider costs other than merchandise costs fixed for the time period involved in merchandise decisions. Price lines are firmly established.

Baker's Men's Shop is located in a college city and is in direct competition with a "better merchandise" departmentalized specialty store. In addition to the owner, there are two other employees, both of whom have been with the firm for fifteen years. Advertising is budgeted at a fixed amount; alterations are made for a fixed monthly fee by a local seamstress; receiving, handling, and marking are done by the two employees. The only cost that the owner can control is merchandise cost. Price lines are maintained at a level consistent with the store's reputation for quality goods. The fixity of costs and price lines do not permit shortrun price-volume experiments.

48

The manager of a departmentalized specialty store prepares special cost studies for some merchandise decisions. The usual objects of these studies are new items and large purchases requiring heavy inventory costs.[3]

Black's, a departmentalized specialty store, is located in a large southern city. The manager developed *ad hoc* incremental cost data for an item—hand-blown glassware—that is new in the city. The analysis indicated that incremental delivery costs would be 25 cents per set. The manager informed the employees that a bonus of 15 cents per set would be paid on every sale which resulted in the consumer carrying the glassware out of the store; such a bonus would be less than the savings in incremental cost.

The manager also used the analysis to establish a price on the glassware lower than in other regions. He recognizes that the lower price can result in a total net dollar contribution greater than that from higher unit prices. The manager indicates that he has chosen a "penetration" instead of a "skimming" price. Lowering prices to attract volume is not an unusual practice in departmentalized stores; but supporting the decision with a quantified analysis is unusual.

Merchandise decisions of store managers are sometimes influenced by "projected estimates of profitability" analyses. Studies of this type are prepared by suppliers of merchandise new to the store. The analyses are based on external information—experiences of similar stores, for example—and seldom rely on internal data.

Accounting data are developed for management in some departmentalized operations. But there is no strong evidence which indicates that such data are important in the examinations of alternatives.

Janet Lea's Department Store maintains an accounting system that develops operating statements for each of 50 departments. The departmental statements are based on the "contribution plan accounting" method which assigns "direct costs" to the

[3] This practice is consistent with that suggested by McNair and May, *Harv. Bus. Rev.,* XXXV, 105-22.

departments. The profitability of departments is gauged by their "contribution" to unassigned indirect costs. Management uses these statements for control; decisions involving departmental changes are not based directly on these reports.

The management of Janet Lea's indicates that decisions to add two large departments were based on analyses prepared by manufacturers of the new merchandise. A decision to relocate a department was based on management's subjective analysis of the situation which extended over several weeks. The merchandise manager stated that monthly statements had indicated that the department was not doing as well as desired. Yet he did not objectively determine the opportunity costs of continued operations. His time was consumed by the routine of retail selling. After several weeks of "mulling it over," he decided to move the department to a new location.

The manner in which the management decided to relocate the department is not unusual. Subjective analyses are often substituted for quantified analyses because of time pressures and the absence of suitable data. The "contribution plan accounting" method is used in the store, but the accounting reports serve decision making only by indicating troublesome departments. A question of relocating a department requires other kinds of data. Specifically, the net incremental revenue from an alternative line of merchandise constitutes the opportunity cost of failure to move a department. Accounting methods cannot develop opportunity cost data; they can indicate the net incremental revenue of the present merchandise line.

THE CASE STUDIES IN TERMS OF RATIONAL DECISION MAKING

The actual uses of accounting described in this chapter can be evaluated in terms of a model for rational decision making. This section does not construct a full mathematical model, but it indicates the principal variables and relationships that would be incorporated in such a model.[4] The analysis is developed briefly with no attempt to supply the magnitudes of the relationships—it is general and applies to all types of retailers. The discussion is accordingly truistic: it outlines a self-evident pattern of logic. The question is how retailers can and do apply the logic in a world of change and uncertainty.

Elements of a prescriptive model

A model for rational retailing decisions would consist of the following elements:

1. Recognition of the need for simultaneous decisions: decisions on product lines, on prices, on advertising and other efforts to differentiate the product, and on the allocation of floor space. The optimum value of any one of these variables depends upon the position of the others. In addition, there are related longrun decisions on expansion and contraction of store space, modernization of the store, and so on. Obviously the simultaneous solution of all the relevant equations is complex, even ignoring problems of uncertainty.

2. Incorporation of the four economic principles of rational decision making. Of these, the discounting principle is least important; pricing, product line, and floor space allocation decisions do not involve sufficient commitments over a period of time to make discounting future revenues important. A rational model must incorporate the other three principles—the incremental principle, the time perspective principle, and the opportunity cost principle. (1) The marginal costs and marginal revenues of each commodity, for all relevant prices and sales efforts, must be considered. This involves estimates of demand elasticities for all commodities, no easy task when hundreds or thousands of items are involved. (2) The impact of today's decisions on the "store image" and the future customer goodwill must

[4] For a more complete mathematical treatment see Bob R. Holdren, *The Structure of a Retail Market and the Market Behavior of Retail Units* (Englewood Cliffs, N. J.: Prentice-Hall, 1960).

be evaluated. (3) The outcomes of all alternative uses of the same space, the same funds and the same personnel must be compared.

Other details add to the complexity of retailing decisions:

1. There are complementary relations in demand. A change in price or selling effort on one item has repercussions on the sales of others.

2. There is the problem of optimum allocation of floor space. Two factors bearing upon this problem are the location of items in relation to the flow of consumer traffic and the quantity of each item to have in current stock. In the allocation of space, retailing has great shortrun flexibility as compared, for example, with manufacturing or with plant nurseries.

3. There must be attention to the rate of stock turnover, an important variable for determining the contribution to the profit of each item; the longer an item stays on the shelves, the less profitable the use of space. The fact that turnover is related to location in the store and to the quantity of the particular item on display stands in the way of a simple solution.

4. There must be an estimation of future markdowns on each item, a serious problem for seasonal and fashion goods.

5. There must be a weighing of sales effort for the store as a whole against effort on individual items. Storewide advertising, for example, must be weighed against advertising particular departments or commodities.

6. There must be attention to the availability of working capital. A shortage of current funds requires greater stress on low investment and high turnover items; sometimes it stimulates markdowns or more active selling efforts.

Many of these considerations are oriented to the market. But optimum retail decisions must also consider costs, incremental costs being the most relevant. For some retailers the cost of goods sold may provide a close approximation of incremental costs. Retail decisions may also involve differentials in inward transportation, handling, delivery, credit, buying, special advertising, and display expenses, and so on. One of the new developments in large-scale retailing is a specialized accounting system, such as merchandising management accounting, to determine those costs and to allocate them on an incremental basis.

The case studies evaluated

The suggested model indicates that a retailer must consider a great number of uncertain factors whenever a decision of consequence is made. No doubt most small retailers recognize the importance of these factors; they also recognize the difficulties of estimating the relevant equations, whether quantitative or qualitative, and solving them simultaneously. To simplify the analysis, small retailers pay particular attention to only a few of the major variables.

Retailers use shortcuts, simplifications, and rules of thumb because of the complexity of the real world; but there is no reason for accepting their actual behavior as the optimum behavior. Indeed, the attention given to a few well-defined variables such as cash, "profit," and gross margins may lead to neglect of less definable but important variables. For example, the retailer who is concerned with the maintenance of liquidity (cash) may ignore the longer run implications of "quick sales" and "closeouts." Information is scarce and frequently uncertain, but the most satisfactory decisions cannot be reached by "happily ignoring" pertinent aspects of a problem.

No doubt, the retail budget based on extrapolation of past sales data is a convenient method for dealing with merchandising decisions. In fact, many small retailers reduce buying decisions to a routine by stocking established merchandise with fixed price lines. The relatively unchanging merchandise mix enables the retailers to rely heavily on analyses born of experience, supported in some stores by historical data. Thus, the retailer reduces the amount of attention to complementary demand relationships, floor space allocations, and product differentiation effort. Retailers use merchandise budgets to implement planned buying with stress on simplicity. And there is every reason to accept the practice as sound. However, retailers may find that their budgets become crutches which, slavishly used, cripple the user. The misuse of budgets is illustrated by the failure to reorder because a category is "bought." Conditions change, and the forecast of demand prepared for the budget may be inappropriate at a later period.

Accounting also involves considerable simplification from the complexities of a complete theoretical model. Usually retail accounting quite correctly avoids the arbitrary and irrelevant overhead allocations found in manufacturing. But retail accounting in small firms also overlooks some incremental costs needed for decisions. The question is whether small firms would benefit from programed incremental analyses; this involves a comparison of benefits and costs. Most small retailers have never heard of incremental accounting methods; others who know something about such methods consider them too costly. Yet they spend money for accounting data which they admit are not used for decisions but are used for control.

Ad hoc cost analyses permit the flexible consideration of factors relevant for particular decisions without the expense of special programing. In actual practice small businessmen come closer to the rational decision-making model in their *ad hoc* analyses, because they are then not bound by the conventions of budgeting and accounting.

IMPLICATIONS FOR PRACTICE

The preceding discussion suggests the following implications for accounting practice:

1. Small retailers with few changes in the accounting system can use accounting data in forecasting, especially for items with stable demands. More complete information on

individual items would be required—for example, detailed breakdowns on volume, prices, cost of goods sold, and price revisions. The small retailer must determine the items with sufficiently stable sales to justify projection.

2. Elaborate incremental systems, such as merchandise management accounting, are too costly for small store use, though these stores can advantageously use incremental concepts in merchandising decisions. Small retailers may well attempt to estimate the incremental cost of stocking, especially if the item is one not previously handled or one which requires an unusually large investment.

3. Quantitative *ad hoc* analyses can be prepared for any decision. Such analyses require subjective judgment about key relationships. Actual pencil-and-paper computations encourage more systematic evaluations of decision alternatives.

4. Of the accounting systems currently used in retailing, net income departmental reporting is the least satisfactory for decision-making purposes because of its reliance on arbitrary allocations. Contribution plan accounting avoids most of those allocations but uses a cost concept (direct cost) which has no necessary relation to variable cost or incremental cost; direct costs in this system refer to zones of responsibility rather than to cost-volume relationships. Some simple form of "marginal income analysis" would be preferable to the usual systems, for it would focus attention on costs affected by decisions.

That small retailers simplify their analysis in making decisions is understandable; the practical world of business is too complex and uncertain to permit the exact application of refined theory. The need is for a compromise between mechanical uses of conventional approaches and flexible evaluations for individual problems. Accounting will continue to play a part in small retailers' decisions, but there is room for experimentation with new methods that meet the needs of decision making more directly.

4

MANUFACTURING FIRMS

SMALL MANUFACTURING firms make three important classes of decisions which are considered in this chapter: (1) product diversification, (2) investment, and (3) pricing. These firms represent a variety of types: special order and continuous production, single and multiple products, keen competition and local monopoly. The central interest of this discussion is the kinds of accounting data that managements use for the analysis of the three types of decisions.

SOME GENERALIZATIONS

The following generalizations apply to accounting and decision making in manufacturing.

1. There is little evidence that accounting data are important to product diversification decisions of firms included in this study. The uncertainties of such decisions, e.g., opportunity costs, demand, and reactions of competitors, are not resolved by accounting data.

2. Investment decisions are based primarily on subjective evaluations, although cost estimates support the analysis on occasion. The firms have programed accounting data for use in recurring replacement decisions, but the programed data are of questionable value.

3. Neither special-order nor continuous-process manufacturers covered by the study use formal job order or process cost accounting. Data from the financial accounts are used to construct special cost studies.

4. Product cost estimates invariably include some provision for overhead. However, many managements, though not familiar with all the refinements of incremental reasoning, make decisions at least partially consistent with marginal analysis.

5. Finally, the status of accounting in pricing decisions is heavily dependent upon market structures within which firms operate. Some market conditions encourage the use of costs as determined by accounting (full costs in the specific firms studied). Other market conditions stimulate flexible adjustment of prices to demand.

PRODUCT DIVERSIFICATION
DECISIONS OF TWO FIRMS

Product-line decisions, especially those to manufacture new products, are crucial. Such decisions commit the firm to a long-range course of action and usually require an investment in fixed facilities. In this section we concentrate on the decisions of two firms to manufacture a new product.

Lake Concrete Products' immediate competitor sold his firm in December, 1959. The new owner of the competing firm manufactured concrete burial vaults (the sole producer in the area) in another plant. Mr. Lake anticipated that this situation could lead to price cutting. He expected that the new management would shade prices on concrete blocks because of the cushion afforded by monopoly profits in burial vaults. Price warfare could only result in lost volume for Lake. He would not retaliate in kind for two reasons: he objected strongly to price shading on ethical grounds, and he was not sure that volume would increase as a result. The need for action became more pronounced when the competing firm published a lowered price schedule to be effective in the spring of 1960.

Mr. Lake considered two alternatives: to manufacture burial vaults or to manufacture septic tanks. His first inclination was to investigate burial vaults. Once he took this approach, he gave no subsequent thought to septic tanks, because the evaluation of burial vaults was encouraging.

Mr. Lake chose the prevailing price ($75.00) established by the monopolist, because he reasoned the competitor would not risk price wars on two fronts. He polled funeral parlor directors on the possible sales of a new vault. They assured him that a new vault would have a market.

The cost calculation assumed the following form:

Materials	$ 5.00
Labor	15.00
	$20.00

Overhead was not included in the calculation because Mr. Lake recognized that it was irrelevant to this decision. Yet he included direct labor in the estimate even though there was idle labor time in the plant. Subjectively, he recognized that a large part of the labor cost was not incremental. The cost calculation therefore reflected only part of his reasoning about costs; it recognized the fixity of overhead but not the fixity of labor cost. Thus the subjective estimate of costs rather than the cost calculation influenced the decision.

Information for the cost calculation was gathered externally; the owner had no previous experience in manufacturing concrete products requiring such large quantities of material. The manufacturer of the molds was the primary source of cost data; demand estimates were obtained from the buyers. Internal sales records revealed information on products selling to an altogether different market; obviously, they could not supply information on a product not yet sold.

Case Concrete Products was stimulated to decision making by the desire of the owner's son to quit college and become an active partner in the firm. Once it was definitely decided that the son would become a partner, Mr. Case was prompted to consider alternative means of increasing profits. Present profits were not sufficient to allow a "reasonable" salary for both men.

Mr. Case got information from various sources; for example, plumbers mentioned that a new line of septic tanks would sell and he saw for himself the amount of building in areas off the sewer lines. In addition to this information, he knew that an expanding market for septic tanks was being supplied by only one producer. At no single time did he attempt to determine all the alternatives that might increase profits, nor did he actively search for information. Rather, the information about one alternative (to manufacture septic tanks) seems to have searched for him.[1]

If the information had been received at any time other than when his son desired a part in the firm, it is doubtful that Mr. Case would have recognized its potentiality. At that particular moment, he was receptive to this kind of information and was persuaded by it to produce septic tanks.

The sole producer had an established price of $65.00. Mr. Case did not know exactly what reaction to expect from the monopolist, but he thought it was reasonable to expect no reaction. On this basis, he established his own price at $65.00. His estimate of cost was:

Materials	$26.85
Labor	9.00
Overhead	3.60
	$39.45

The materials cost estimate was precise: it was based on the owner's previous experience with concrete and the requirements of the Board of Health. Labor cost was based on estimates of man-hours required to pour and strip each septic tank. Overhead was applied at the standard rate of 10 percent of prime costs. The calculation represented an estimate of the full costs of a septic tank.

[1] Cyert, *et al.*, suggest a "mating theory of search" to explain the way proposals are brought to management's attention. See Richard M. Cyert, W. R. Dill, and James G. March, "The Role of Expectations in Business Decisions," *Administrative Science Quarterly*, III (Dec., 1958), 338.

Several significant observations can be made concerning the cost estimate. First, Mr. Case recognized that labor was fixed, since the tank was to be manufactured with excess capacity. He also recognized that the overhead was fixed (except for a small amount of user cost of the molds). Thus, net incremental revenue for each tank was actually about $38.15 per tank, although not actually calculated. However, he anticipated that a great deal of profit could be realized at the price of $65.00.

A second observation is that the cost analysis was made *after* the decision to manufacture septic tanks. It appears that the calculation simply verified certain previously conceived notions of the relationship between costs and production of septic tanks. There is doubt that the calculation was important in making the decision.

There are similarities between the decision-making processes of both firms: (1) both decisions involved a new activity; (2) in both firms the decision-making processes were stimulated by external events; (3) the analyses were influenced by information that was available and relevant to one alternative; and (4) quantifications of the analyses occurred after the courses of action had been selected and actually played only a small part in the decisions.

Significantly, accounting data were not used at any crucial phase in the decisions to establish new product lines. Accounting data, however, result from systems designed to handle an already established production scheme and, therefore, cannot furnish pertinent data regarding any radical departure from that scheme.[2] When striking out on a new path, the decision maker must rely on external sources for information.

[2] Case Concrete Products manufactured burial vaults and miscellaneous concrete products prior to the decision. The decision involved a product that was subject to entirely different demand characteristics but somewhat similar cost characteristics. Lake Concrete Products likewise was geared to produce for one type of market (construction) whereas burial vaults involved different demand and cost characteristics.

INVESTMENT DECISIONS OF TWO FIRMS

The role of accounting in investment decisions is to provide data which (1) indicate the need for a decision, (2) are useful for comparative analyses, and (3) check the accuracy of estimates so that future decisions can benefit from past errors. The decisions discussed in the foregoing section, which in a sense are investment decisions as well as product diversification decisions, indicate that some small firms do not use accounting data for all three purposes. Indeed, only in rare circumstances is it possible for a firm to program the data which are necessary to fulfill all the requirements for decision making.

Some firms anticipate regularly recurring investment decisions and therefore accumulate data specifically for such decisions.

Ro-Na-Readi-Mix Concrete maintains cost records for each truck in its fleet. These records include the costs of maintenance, repairs, gas, oil, grease, etc., and are bases for control reports. Management stated that the records are useful for replacement decisions in that trucks becoming overly expensive to operate are brought to the attention of management. But the cost records are not important in actual replacement decisions; management indicated that the firm's financial condition and prospects for the future are the important determinants.

Three other ready-mixed concrete firms included in this study accumulate cost data on individual trucks. However, trucks are seldom replaced solely on the basis of the programed data. More important to the firms are financial considerations: a fully equipped concrete delivery truck costs approximately $16,000, a sizable expenditure. The cost records provide some means for effecting cost control, but they are not useful for comparing alternatives.

These companies probably would not benefit from great refinement in replacement analyses. Smith's intensive study of a large trucking firm indicates that truck replacement decisions are not improved significantly by decision rules based on the optimum replacement time.[3] Smith states that "trucking firms, and perhaps business firms generally, are not likely to follow replacement policies that deviate seriously from optimal policies."[4] The ready-mixed concrete producers do not replace trucks according to inflexible decision rules. In fact, the criterion of postponability (delaying consideration of less urgent decisions) which governs truck replacements may produce results as economical as would more refined analysis.

Some replacement decisions instead of being repetitive occur but few times in the life of a firm.

A *Clay Refractory* mines a special clay which is processed and sold to firebrick manufacturers. A large scoop shovel, used to mine the clay, had incurred extensive repairs resulting in costly delays. A supplier was contacted and an analysis was made of a proposed replacement costing $50,000. Assuming that the analysis was correct, the new equipment would reduce mining costs by twenty cents per ton and would pay out in four years.

The cost estimates used in the comparative cost study were based on information supplied by the manufacturer and by the financial accounts. The manufacturer estimated operating results based on other users' experience and on engineering studies; the refractory management made estimates of costs that would be incurred if the old shovel were kept. Management recognized that the book value of the present shovel was no indication of its current value. Some cost data supplied by the accounts were relevant, e.g., repair and maintenance cost, whereas others were not, e.g., depreciation. Management accepted the relevant costs and rejected the irrelevant.

The experiences of these two firms indicate that (1) in some firms, data programed for repetitive replacement de-

[3] Vernon L. Smith, "Economic Equipment Policies: An Evaluation," *Management Science*, IV (Oct., 1957), 20-37. Reprinted in Edward H. Bowman and Robert B. Fetter, *Analyses of Industrial Operations* (Homewood, Ill.: Richard D. Irwin, Inc., 1959), pp. 444-62.

[4] Bowman and Fetter, 460.

cisions may be useful for management control but are unimportant in the actual decision to replace a specific asset, but (2) in other firms, financial accounting statements provide a source of data which, when used correctly, are helpful for the analysis of replacement decisions.

There is little difference between the problem of choosing among a number of new assets and that of replacing old assets: comparative data are required for both kinds of analysis. However, a firm can rarely anticipate investment decisions such as expansion, renovation, and innovation. Accounting data are of little help in such decisions. Original thinking and new sources of data must aid the appraisal of a course of action not previously taken by the firm. But the next case illustrates how accounting can perform a function in decision making in general, even when it has little direct effect on any single decision.

Lake Concrete Products installed a new product line requiring a sizable initial investment. *Subsequently*, Mr. Lake maintains records of sales and costs of the new product. The intent of this practice is to check the accuracy of estimates and to learn from mistakes.

Although Mr. Lake may never again make a product-line decision of this sort, he recognizes that his predictive ability is important for successful operation. Accounting provides means by which learning from experience can be made a part of the firm's routine.

PRICING DECISIONS OF FOUR FIRMS

The small firms included in this study differ in the extent to which they adhere to a full-cost plus a markup basis in pricing. Some firms adhere rigidly to the full-cost basis; others emphasize demand and market conditions in pricing decisions. In this section, we examine these various patterns of behavior, using cases as illustrations.

Full costs rigidly used

A concrete product manufacturer has a local monopoly on some products, but the manager prices all products on the basis of full cost plus 100 percent. The owner maintains a card file in which he records the full cost of each product; when the firm's costs increase, the owner spreads the increase over all products and announces a new price schedule.

When asked why he bases prices solely on cost without consideration of demand, the owner replied that he requires every product to "carry its fair share of overhead." He evaluates the profitability of each product on the basis of its return in excess of direct costs plus allocated overhead. Underlying this policy is, perhaps, an unsophisticated recognition of opportunity costs; if each product is recovering its share of overhead, then the fixed facilities are being optimally allocated among the various products.

A second reason for not differentiating prices on the basis of demand is the owner's concern for his reputation as a "fair" businessman. Over the years the owner has presented a consistent and stable basis for prices to the public; he fears that any other method of pricing would destroy the customer relations that he enjoys. He recognizes that an inelastic demand exists for many of his products, but raising prices to take advantage of the situation would be inconsistent with his basic policy of "fairness."

Full costs used with some flexibility

A building materials (precast stone) manufacturer prepares estimates of full costs for bidding purposes. The estimates invariably include nonincremental overhead cost allocations in addition to labor and materials. However, the markup varies according to each job and, in many instances, the price is below full costs. The firm is trying to build up a market, and the management believes that it must evaluate each prospective contract on an individual basis.

The full-cost estimates serve only as a starting point in pricing; the firm would willingly take a contract at less than full costs if the customer offered possibilities for future sales. If there is little information available on potential future sales, or if it is a competitively bid contract, the firm will insist that the price be at least full cost. This case study is consistent with Bartschi's findings of widespread use of full-cost estimates in the precast stone industry.[5] But the case suggests that full-cost estimates are only a first step in pricing decisions.

Full costs with complete adjustment to competition

A ready-mixed concrete producer prepared an *ad hoc* study of product costs for use in a decision to lower the price schedule. A new firm had recently entered the market with a price somewhat less than the stabilized market price. The firm examined the income statements and made special studies of truck operating costs to determine the full cost of delivered concrete. When the study of costs was completed, the firm published a new schedule in which the unit prices were greater than both full-cost and the new entrant's prices. The firm found that it still could not compete with the new one; others in the market were lowering their prices, putting added pressure on the management. The firm lowered its prices; the re-revised price schedule was, with few exceptions, identical to that of the new entrant's and below full costs. In this case, the pricing decision started with an estimate of full costs, but demand and competitor's actions were the principal determinants of the final outcome.

Full costs not used

A concrete block manufacturer mentioned earlier prepared an estimate of incremental costs when deciding upon the price of a new product. The owner searched for information on prospective demand and competitors' reactions. The final price resulted only after the owner considered both incremental costs and demand.

[5] Donald P. Bartschi, "Costing Pre-Cast Stone for Estimating and Control," *N.A.C.A. Bulletin*, XXXVII (Jan., 1956), 644-7.

The owner does not know the full cost of the firm's major products—concrete and cinder blocks. The market for building blocks during the construction season is very competitive and prices fluctuate as the several firms in the market attempt to maintain volume. The owner does know the approximate incremental cost of building blocks, since it consists only of materials; labor costs are fixed for the entire year. The owner takes contracts that he thinks yield only a few cents per block in excess of incremental costs. In this highly competitive market, full cost means nothing to the firm's owner; his principal concerns in pricing decisions are incremental cost, demand, and competitive prices.

Evaluation of the pricing practices

The case studies indicate a variety of practices in using cost data for pricing decisions. Full-cost estimates may be the sole determinant of price, or they may serve only as a starting point. But the question remains: why do firms calculate full costs? The weaknesses and limitations of cost data requiring arbitrary allocations of overhead are well recognized in the literature: "it is necessary to recognize the fact that cost allocation at the best is loaded with assumption and that in many cases highly arbitrary methods of apportionment are employed in practice. Certainly it is wise not to take the results of the usual process of internal cost imputation seriously."[6] In spite of such pronouncements, firms continue to make full-cost estimates.

P. J. D. Wiles indicates that there are several explanations for the practice of full-cost pricing:[7] (1) firms are ignorant of demand elasticities and in this ignorance they will stick to any price that proves to be profitable; (2) the outcome of price experiments are uncertain and this un-

[6] William A. Paton and A. C. Littleton, *An Introduction to Corporate Accounting Standards* (New York: American Accounting Association, 1940), p. 120.

[7] *Price, Cost and Output* (Oxford: Basil Blackwell, 1961), pp. 47-8.

certainty alone is sufficient to keep the firm's "playing safe"; (3) frequent changes in volume (resulting from price changes) are impracticable for production planning; (4) frequent price changes can result in loss of customer goodwill; and (5) a period of constant prices is necessary to estimate demand; firms prefer to hold an established price for a season and, if sales are low, they lower the price the following season. All these explanations are, in some way, applicable to the firms in this study which rigidly apply full cost plus a predetermined markup.

Wiles ignores the explanation that by charging each product with a share of the fixed facility cost, the firm is attempting to determine the opportunity cost. This explanation is borne out by the desire of the firm that every product should carry its share of the overhead. Carl T. Devine denies that firms are able to measure opportunity costs by allocating overhead, since the true measure of a product's profitability is its contribution to fixed costs.[8] There is no reason that an overhead allocation will give the correct measurement of opportunity cost when excess capacity exists; at the other extreme, such allocations do not measure the opportunity costs in the case of great pressure of many alternatives on limited capacity. Thus overhead allocations almost inevitably overstate or understate the true opportunity costs.

From a practical standpoint, the building up of prices from full-cost data sidesteps some of the uncertainties of demand and market reactions. However, a rigid application of full costs in a market which does not allow such a naive approach could be disastrous. The cases indicate that small firms do adjust to demand and competition.

To summarize, the presence of full-cost estimates does not mean that the pricing decisions rest solely on costs. The firm can and does make adjustments to demand conditions; but if the firm can ignore demand in pricing, full costs plus

[8] "Cost Accounting and Pricing Policies," *Accounting Review*, XXV (Oct., 1950), 384-9. Reprinted in Thomas, pp. 333-41.

a markup provide a stable, consistent basis for prices in the face of uncertainty.

IMPLICATIONS FOR PRACTICE

The discussion of the role of accounting in product-line, investment, and pricing decisions leads to the following suggestions.

1. Small manufacturing firms can use periodic studies of product costs more practicably than integrated cost systems in decision making.[9] The cost of full-fledged cost accounting systems is prohibitive. Management can make *ad hoc* cost studies quickly and easily; an added advantage of special studies is that management will not be tempted to use cost data that are readily available but that are incorrect for the particular problem being considered.

2. Small manufacturing firms could use marginal income analysis in preparing periodic cost studies. The information would be helpful in firms operating in highly competitive markets, since it would indicate the floor for prices. Firms operating in less competitive markets and presently pricing on the basis of full-cost estimates would find marginal income information extremely valuable in product-line adjustment and evaluation decisions. A decision to drop a line, for example, must include estimates of escapable costs and revenues; this kind of information is available if marginal income analysis is used. Otherwise, if the firm employs full-cost data, the management must separate the incremental cost from the sunk cost.[10]

3. Small manufacturing firms should maintain selected accounting data, especially the kinds of information that

[9] This suggestion is supported by Edward S. Thompson, "A Program for Profitable Use of Costs in a Small Factory," *N.A.A. Bulletin*, XL (Jan., 1959), 53.
[10] Thompson, *ibid.*, p. 55, and John W. Christie, "A Concrete Products Company Uses Direct Costing with Standard Costs," *N.A.C.A. Bulletin*, XXXVIII (Jan., 1957), 690 prescribe marginal income analysis for small firms.

would enable management to follow up the results of decisions. Investment decisions involve projections of future revenues and costs; firms could check the accuracy of their estimates by accumulating the data and comparing the results with the forecasts. If the decision is reversible, management has solid information on which to base its subsequent action; if the decision is irreversible, management can note its errors and improve future decision making.

5

PRINTING FIRMS

*I*N THE CONTEXT of printing, we take up an issue which has broad implications for industries in general: under what circumstances is it advantageous to program accounting data for one kind of decision? The discussion of this issue is based on an analysis of three topics: (1) the implications of accounting methods which develop cost data for pricing decisions; (2) case studies of pricing decisions of actual printing firms, with emphasis on the role of accounting; and (3) the use of *ad hoc* economic analysis for other types of decisions.

SOME GENERALIZATIONS

We start with some generalizations based both upon the literature on printing industry accounting and upon the case studies.

1. There is a movement in the industry, led by trade associations and large printing firms, which encourages printers to determine accurately the "cost of doing business."[1] The full cost of individual jobs is considered by proponents of the movement to be the important consideration in pricing decisions. Accounting systems are designed to produce full-cost data.

2. Printers are incapable of recovering the full cost of every job. Competitive pressures prevent strict adherence to "full cost plus profit" bases in pricing decisions. The accounting determination of full costs serves little purpose in some decisions except to establish a floor (albeit flexible) below which prices should not fall.

3. In large firms, accounting is an important tool for cost control. This function of accounting is closely related to the size of the firm. Smaller firms of three to six employees rely on management supervision for cost control.

4. The homeostatic function of accounting is evident in several case studies. The practice of revising hourly cost rates on the basis of reported net income illustrates this function of accounting. Control systems in some printing firms develop measures which play a part in the homeostatic process. Some firms experiment with standard cost systems; others use less refined control methods.

5. Accounting data are not used in equipment replace-

---

[1] In a series of articles appearing in an industry newsletter, *Printing Impressions* (March-July, 1960), Theodore P. Von Bosse reports that prices on a hypothetical job on which printers were asked to bid covered a wide range. This variation, the author states, is an indication that printers do not "know their costs." Von Bosse ignores demand as an important price determinant, especially the fact that demand elasticities differ in the various markets in which the respondents operate.

ment decisions. In fact, little quantitative analysis is used in decisions of this type. Accounting cost systems may influence the decisions by indicating the inefficiencies of continued operation of the equipment.

PRINTING INDUSTRY
ACCOUNTING METHODS

One purpose of cost accounting methods in the printing industry is to develop information for use in the pricing decision.[2] Current literature maintains that "job cost plus profit equals selling price."[3] This literature expounds on the proposition that "full cost" is the relevant concept of cost to use in pricing decisions. Accounting methods are designed to develop the full cost of every order going through a job print shop. In order to understand the accounting techniques used in printing, it is necessary to outline the processes required to produce printed matter.

The production flow

Figure 3 is a simplified representation of the work performed by most printers.[4] Every job must go through some or all of these processes. (1) An order is received by a printer. The customer specifies what is to be printed, how it is to be printed, and how much is to be printed. (2) Materials are requisitioned from the stockroom and specifications are sent to the composing room. (3) In the composing room, the printed material is reproduced in a form required by the particular press on which the work is to be done.[5] (4) A

[2] Although accounting methods in printing firms serve other purposes, the literature and interviewees stress the importance of this purpose.

[3] Peter Becker, Jr., *Managing Your Business* (Washington, D. C.: Printing Industry of America, 1959), p. 14.

[4] This diagram is based partly on a figure in William Green, "Wellesley Press, Inc.," a Harvard Business School Case (Intercollegiate Case Clearing House Index No. 3C9, 1958).

[5] The flow diagram assumes a letterpress operation. To convert the diagram to one applying to an offset press, substitute "offset plates" for "galley."

Figure 3. Production flow diagram for a small printshop

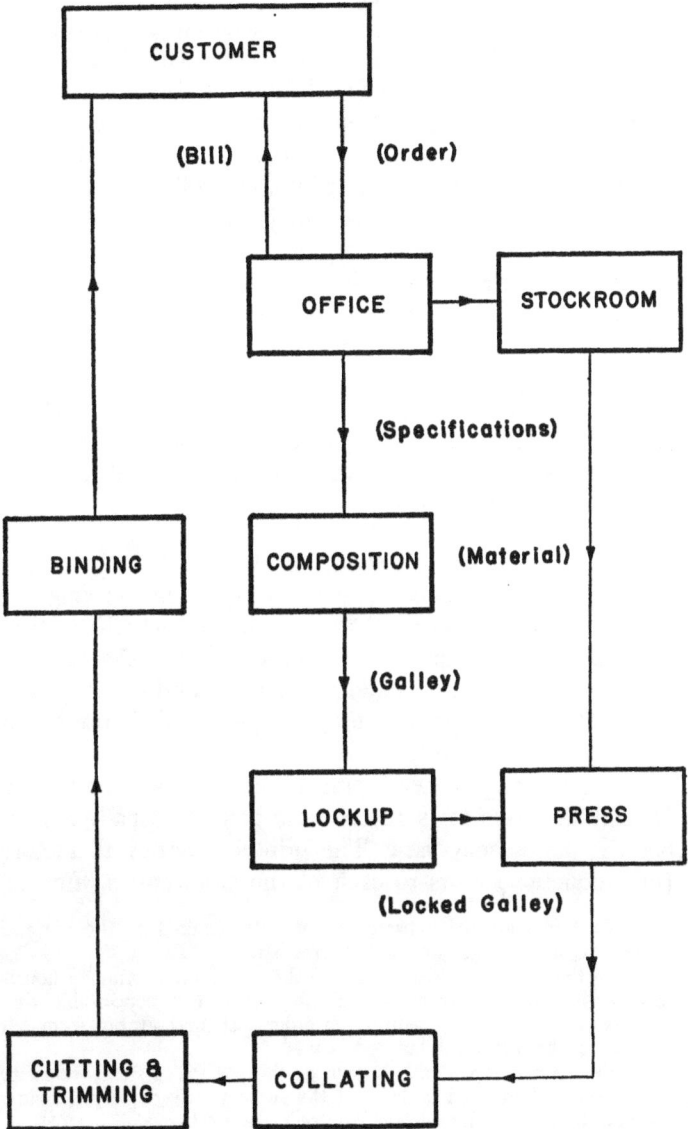

73

"galley proof" is made up in the composing room and sent to the customer for approval. (5) If the customer approves, the type is "locked up," i.e., various operations are performed to ready the galley for use in the press. (6) The locked galley is taken to the press, which produces the order in the desired quantities. (7) The job leaves the pressroom and receives whatever additional work is necessary. Cutting and trimming are necessary on most jobs, but collating and binding are required only for part of the jobs.

To estimate the cost of a particular job, the printer determines the extent to which the costs of each production process (materials, composing, presswork, cutting, collating, etc.) adhere to the job as it passes through the plant. A job is costed on the basis of the time taken to go through each of the processes (hereafter called "cost centers").[6] There are two principal accounting methods by which cost data are obtained: the all-inclusive hour cost method and the factory-hour cost method.[7]

All-inclusive hour cost method

This method of costing printed matter is receiving the most attention in current literature and in actual practice. Its present status is largely due to the efforts of the Printing Industry of America (a trade association) and other spokesmen. The method is simple and requires only a minimum of computational effort.

The first step in developing all-inclusive hour costs is to forecast the costs for a future time period[8]—usually a year, but the period may vary. The printer allocates all factory (or production) costs to each of the cost centers. For ex-

[6] Cost of materials is based on quantity required by the job and is not a "cost center" as we use the term here.

[7] In this discussion, we emphasize the use of predetermined hourly costs as the method for obtaining job costs. It is conceivable that printers can and do use a simple job order cost method, but from our experience, the method is not widely used.

[8] One system (popularly known as the "MYB" system) refers to such costs as "budgeted costs" and the subsequently developed hourly costs are termed "budgeted hourly rates." See Becker.

74

ample, a particular press is charged with the depreciation of the press and a portion of plant depreciation (based on floor space), the wages of the pressmen, and other factory overhead items on some "reasonable" basis. Total factory costs for the ensuing period are thus determined for each cost center. Selling and administrative expenses are allocated to each cost center based on the relationship of total selling and administrative expense to factory expense. For example, if total expected factory costs are $10,000 and total expected selling and administrative costs are $3,000, an additional 30 cents is allocated to the cost center for every $1.00 factory cost. The result is total cost for each cost center for the coming period.

It is now necessary to determine the hour costs. To do this, the printer estimates the number of hours that each cost center is to be in operation and how much of this time is "chargeable" to the customer.[9] Estimated chargeable hours for each cost center are divided into total cost of that cost center, resulting in "all-inclusive hour cost."

To price a job, the time spent in each productive process is multiplied by the hourly cost of the process and the result is added to the cost of materials; a profit margin is added to this total.

Factory-hour cost method

Factory-hour cost determination requires the same general calculations as all-inclusive hour costs. However, the resultant hourly costs include only the direct factory costs—no attempt is made to allocate selling and administrative costs to cost centers. Using this method, a printing job is priced as follows: (1) time spent in each cost center is multiplied by the factory-hour rate; (2) to this figure is added the cost of materials; (3) to this total is added an

[9] Subtracting nonchargeable hours (the total of time spent on activities for which a customer cannot be billed) from the total hours that a cost center is to be in operation results in an estimate of chargeable hours (time spent on activities for which a customer can be billed).

amount (percentage markup on cost) to "cover selling, administrative expenses, and profit."

A legitimate question that can be asked at this point is why we find these two methods in use. A recent article in a trade journal contrasts these two methods in terms of advantages and disadvantages.[10] The author, E. T. Leverenz, lists these advantages of the all-inclusive cost method: it is a tried method familiar to all printers; and it requires less detail, since it is not necessary to use additional percentages to absorb selling and administrative costs (when pricing the job). The disadvantages of the system are: (1) the cost of handling materials (a factory overhead account) is spread over all cost centers and charged to each job. When the customer furnishes certain materials, he is charged handling cost even though no such cost is incurred.[11] (2) There is no opportunity for standardization or comparison of costs within the industry. Selling and administrative costs vary so that hour costs are different from plant to plant. (3) There is no provision for ascertaining the costs of outside purchases. (On some jobs, printers must "farm out" some of the work and the anticipated costs of handling and financing these purchases are spread over all cost centers.)

Leverenz prefers factory-hour costs. He argues that selling and administrative functions are separate cost centers and that all segments of the business should "stand on their own feet." Some jobs require more selling and administrative effort than others; the factory-hour method permits differentiation of overhead cost allocations.

Hour costs and decision making

The data produced by the all-inclusive hour cost method are estimates of full cost—of the average total cost for each chargeable hour. Marginal economic analysis suggests that

[10] E. T. Leverenz, "Pricing Policy," *Graphic Arts Monthly*, XXXI (Sept., 1959), 8-12.
[11] The author suggests that "handling costs" be set up as a separate cost center and not treated as overhead.

such data are inappropriate for pricing decisions, for they stress full costs rather than incremental costs.

Once a printing firm is committed to a rate of output, the cost function is insensitive to small changes in output. The sensitivity to upward changes depends a great deal on how close the printer is to capacity, but unless there is a dramatic change in output, costs are relatively fixed. The only variable elements of a printing job are materials and some factory costs (and selling costs if salesmen are on a commission basis). In fact, case studies suggest that variable costs are between 30 percent and 50 percent of total costs for shortrun changes in output. This indicates that all-inclusive hour costs are far removed from the incremental cost of a particular job; factory-hour costs more nearly approximate incremental cost. But neither method develops incremental data. Why then are such data used in pricing? This question can be evaluated after we examine case materials.

CASE STUDIES OF THE ROLE OF ACCOUNTING IN DECISION MAKING

The seven firms fall into three categories based on organizational considerations. At one extreme, decisions result from the interaction of several persons within the organization; that is, specialization is evident in varying degrees. At the other extreme, decisions emanate from one source, that is, there is only one "decider." Between these two extremes, there are firms which employ some specialization in the decision-making process.

A firm with specialized decision-making processes

We start with the largest printing firm—one with considerable specialization in management.

Phillips Printing Firm is located in a large midwestern city and employs approximately 200 persons. Although the firm is in keen competition with some 75 printers of various sizes, there is some differentiation of product based on quality, service, and location.

The company considers the full cost (as determined by all-inclusive hour costs) of each job to be the floor on pricing. This floor is determined by estimators, who anticipate the time to be consumed in each cost center. As the job is scheduled through the plant, it is accompanied by a "tracer" which records the actual costs. Upon completion of jobs, actual and estimated costs are compared. If a job is subject to a firm bid, the comparison of actual costs with estimated costs serves only as a control device (both production efficiency and the accuracy of estimators are checked). If a job is nonbid (i.e., priced when finished), the tracer provides information for pricing. A markup schedule categorizes jobs into five types. This schedule reflects demand and competition. Higher markups are applied to jobs which are "first runs" or which involve a great deal of "creativity."

Accounting data are not used in other major decisions (equipment replacement, product-line decisions, etc.) except as control data which call attention to inefficient operations. Equipment replacement decisions are highly subjective, often governed by the criterion of postponability.

There are three important control reports for each cost center; these reports are designed to show the following relationships: (1) actual hour costs and predetermined hour costs—the hour costs may be revised if predetermined costs are out of line with actual costs; (2) chargeable hours and nonchargeable hours—this report enables the firm to set efficiency standards for each center; (3) standard time reports—the firm is in the process of establishing standard times, aimed toward establishing a standard cost system and routine cost estimating.

This firm prices on the basis of full cost for various reasons: (1) management considers it unethical to price at less; (2) price shading for some orders could destroy the goodwill that this firm has established; (3) low profit jobs may interfere with scheduling high profit orders. Management recognizes that the incremental costs of a job are low in printing and that this is a reason for keen price competition, yet rejects flexible pricing as basically unsound.

Two firms with less specialized decision-making processes

The two cases cited in this section are comparable in size and in pricing policies. They are in competition with approximately twenty other small job printers. Their practices and policies concerning accounting and pricing decisions are similar and can be discussed concurrently.

Tracy Printing Company and *Hunt Lithographers* specialize in small job order printing; they do not undertake exceptionally long run jobs. The managements of both firms indicate that the majority of their business is on a nonbid basis, i.e., prices are determined only after jobs are completed. On bid contracts of significant size, the quoted price often results from conferences between salesmen and management.

Both firms invariably use "all-inclusive hour costs" as a base for prices. Neither firm has established a schedule of markups; rather, the markup varies according to management's idea about competitive conditions.

Both firms are active promoters of common accounting systems for all small printers. The managements of both firms express the philosophy that each job must cover full costs.

Control techniques are not used extensively. The accounting systems have not been developed to the extent that cost control data flow routinely to management; cost control depends upon supervision rather than reports. The efficiency of individual cost centers is gauged by the ability of the centers to cover their full costs. The focus of attention on allocated costs is consistent with the full-cost philosophy.

As in the Phillips Printing case, accounting data are used in pricing decisions. Accounting determination of full costs establishes the lower limit on price; demand considerations are reflected in the profit markup. Tracers accompany each job (as in Phillips), making possible a comparison of estimated costs and actual costs for control. Hourly costs are reviewed and revised once a year when annual financial statements are available.

Nonprice decisions are based primarily on data other than those developed by the accounting systems. Equipment replacement decisions, for example, result from subjective analysis. They require estimates of future technological change which are difficult to quantify because of great uncertainty. Similarly, some make or buy decisions rest primarily on nonquantitative analyses. For example, Tracy

Printing decided to "farm out" binding to a distant firm, based on an estimate of opportunity costs. Management "felt" that the space occupied by the binding department could be used more profitably in other operations. No attempt was made to quantify the opportunity cost.

Three firms with one-man decision makers

In this section, we discuss three firms, one of which competes in the same market as Phillips Printing, one competes actively with Tracy and Hunt, and the third operates in a small-town duopoly situation.

Wall's Printing Firm specializes in small jobs which are of the type usually ignored by Phillips Printing. The owner's philosophy of pricing is strongly inclined toward full cost. All-inclusive cost rates are used by the owner to arrive at price. The hourly costs determined by the accounting system are compared with published regional rates; if the firm's cost rates are too high or too low as compared with the published rates, the latter may be used in pricing. The owner resists reductions of price below levels indicated by full costs, but makes rare exceptions. Accounting data provide some means of validating cost estimates of individual jobs—although comparison of actual costs with estimated costs is not done systematically.

Kitty-Hawk Printing adopted the all-inclusive cost method only six months prior to the case interview. Before adoption, the owner relied heavily on a regional selling rates manual and subjective judgment. Adoption of the method resulted in an increase in the overall price structure with little loss of regular customers and increased income for the six months. However, strict application of data secured from accounting is impossible. For example, one cost center has, by accounting determination, a cost rate twice that of other firms in the market. Rather than risk pricing on this basis, the rate was lowered in line with competition. This firm has not adopted all the refinements of the system; cost control is not yet afforded by the system.

Independent Lithographer is located in a small town and competes with one other firm. Although Independent Lithographer and the other firm have tacitly agreed to segregate the market into two parts, each firm must still anticipate the reaction of the other to individual pricing decisions. The owner of Independent recognizes this interdependence and estimates carefully the cost and demand characteristics of each job. As the owner stated, hourly costs would be useless unless they were similarly estimated in both firms.

Evaluation of the pricing practices in the cases

The case studies suggest that there are good reasons for the policy of full costs in the printing industry.

1. Printing firms make large numbers of pricing decisions on orders that are highly diverse. The demand conditions vary greatly from one order to another; in addition, there is great uncertainty about demand itself. An individual analysis of incremental revenue and cost on each order is expensive and of doubtful use. The way in which printing firms simplify pricing decisions is to use mechanical accounting techniques for determining full costs and to add markups to those costs. In this way they circumvent much of the problem of uncertainty and the difficulties of measurement.

2. Most firms in the market recognize that the demand for printed matter is relatively inelastic. High prices throughout the industry could result in more profit for the individual firm. Printing firms hope that the widespread use of full costs will limit price competition and permit higher profits for the whole industry. There are firms which do not think in such industrywide terms; these firms perceive immediate profit opportunities to be gained from pricing incrementally, recognizing that out-of-pocket costs of a single job are very low. The supporters of full-cost pricing are trying to bring these "price cutters" into line by encouraging the use of common accounting methods.

3. The awareness that price competition is "not so good" for the individual firm is expressed in ethical objections to price shading (and to price gouging). Full costs provide a standard against which the price behavior of firms can be evaluated; no doubt many printers avoid prices that violate that standard.

4. Many printers believe that consistent references to

full costs in pricing contribute to customer goodwill and thus to volume and profits. Greater flexibility might lead to customer objections to "unfair" discrimination.

There are, however, arguments against too much stress on full costs. A completely mechanical application of predetermined markups on full costs would preclude any adjustment to market forces; most printers vary their markups from one category of business to another and from job to job. In other words they do not push full-cost reasoning to the extreme. There must also be doubt that attempts to limit competition through full-cost formulas can work. Such formulas do not prevent the entry of new firms; they do not keep existing firms with excess capacity from shading prices to get business that contributes to overhead.

In other words, full-cost formulas provide only a partial solution to the problem of pricing in printing. It is easy to understand the stress on full costs in the industry; it is also understandable that there is not complete adherence to those costs.

ROUTINIZED DECISION MAKING VERSUS *AD HOC* ANALYSIS

Printers use two approaches to decision making. One is to rely heavily on programed data; the discussion so far has stressed programed full costs for pricing. The alternative is to rely on nonprogramed analyses. The use of such *ad hoc* analysis is illustrated in two decisions in a printing firm that was closely observed over a period of years by one of the interviewers.

The Forkland Printing Company is now nonexistent, but at the time these decisions were made, it was an active firm in a large competitive market. The accounting system was maintained primarily for financial reports, which indicated that the company was barely breaking even. Pricing decisions were based primarily on a manual of regional hour rates. The pricing policy was full cost plus a fixed markup, but hour cost data were not produced by the accounting system.

Decisions on the size of the sales force. The company's sales force consisted of the full-time efforts of a sales manager and the part-time efforts of the president and vice president. At one time a salesman was hired, but he subsequently was the subject of a problem debated by the board of directors. There was a group of directors which felt that this salesman was uneconomical. These directors pointed out that the salesman's commission was considerably below his guarantee and that this situation was surely unprofitable.

Economic analysis suggests that more serious thought to the size of the force would have been justified and that the issue should have been *expansion* rather than *contraction* of the sales force. One board member made an *ad hoc* analysis of the financial statements which included an estimate that variable costs were roughly 50 percent of the total cost and of revenue. He also pointed out that the company had idle capacity. His analysis, shown below, suggests that a low volume of *added* sales would have justified the employment of an additional salesman.

Estimated incremental revenue		$20,000
Incremental cost of printing	$10,000	
Incremental salesman's guarantee and travel expense	5,000	
Incremental Cost		15,000
Net Incremental Revenue		$5,000

This estimate indicates that an added salesman would have contributed $5,000 to fixed cost and profits of this company. Even with sales as low as $10,000 per year, the company would break even.

It was a mistake for the company to ignore the possibility of additional salesmen, assuming that the "tailor-made" cost and revenue analysis was valid. True enough, the cost data were taken from financial accounting statements—statements which were not designed to provide such data. Even if the income statement had been arranged to show variable and fixed elements of cost, additional analysis would have been required. The salesman's guarantee would have been an incremental cost, but an income statement would have classified it as fixed.

Decisions on the sale or liquidation of the company. Since the company was not particularly profitable, it occurred to one director that liquidation or sale might be desirable. He pointed out that the expenses of the company were understated from the opportunity cost point of view. The most important example was depreciation on the building, which was recorded in the accounts at almost nothing. The building was fifty years old and only certain improvements were being depreciated. The rental value of the building was at least $500 per month. The company was sacrificing the opportunity to earn this rental by remaining in printing. Similarly, the depreciation on the equipment reflected original costs, neglecting the higher replacement costs that would be necessary if the firm were to stay in business. In short, the accounting statements were grossly misleading. They led to a false sense of complacency by concealing the fact that the company was losing money from an economic point of view.

Opportunity cost reasoning led to the sale of the company, a decision that was certainly sound. The only alternative would have been a sharp change in the technology or management, neither of which seemed likely in view of the financial stress.

The accounts appear to have been of little help in this decision, aside from listing the assets and the expense categories. It is of interest, however, that the sale price was at book value. All parties to the sale recognized that the book value was out of touch with current realities, but the accounting figure offered a reference point for a compromise. Thus accounts may serve an important function by providing something definite to which decisions can be referred. When decision makers are confused by a multitude of variables involving much uncertainty, it is understandable that they may turn to something that appears to be "definite," even though in theory it may be quite irrelevant.

INDUSTRY COMPARISONS

It is unnecessary to construct a prescriptive model for printing, but an indication of the ways in which the environment conditioning decision making in printing is similar to or different from that in nurseries and retailing may explain the diversity in decision processes from industry to industry.

Production characteristics

The production characteristics in printing differ from those in nurseries and retail establishments. As compared with the nurseries, printing involves shortrun rather than longrun flexibility in production; the equipment and plant layout permit a rapid shift from one kind of production to another. In printing, decisions on product mix are not so much concerned with conjectural estimates of long-distant future events. Most printing costs, such as material and labor costs, can be estimated with some accuracy prior to actual production. It is possible to develop definite procedures by which "costs" can be estimated, as is shown in the case studies. The existence of cost estimates that appear to have some substance influences management to give them more attention.

When it comes to longrun decisions, such as the purchase of new equipment, the uncertainty is equally great in both printing firms and nurseries; it is not surprising that managers in both industries make use of subjective estimates and rules of thumb on such decisions.

The production characteristics of printing are more like those in retailing, in which there is also a great deal of flexibility in product mix. Retailers, like printers, can shift rapidly from one product variation to another. In both industries, flexibility is limited by the layout and by the company's reputation for special products. The flexibility arises in different ways, however; in printing it involves a change in the mix of work flowing through the plant; in retailing it involves a change in the items displayed on the shelves in a single location.

Variable costs are a smaller proportion of total costs in printing than in retailing; labor costs are relatively fixed for shortrun changes in volume. In retailing, variable costs include wholesale costs which are from half to two-thirds of the total. One might expect that prices would be more flexible in printing, because of the greater proportional difference between price and incremental cost. There are several reasons why this is not the case.

1. The inventory situation is different in the two industries. Retailers invest a large proportion of their capital in inventory and are therefore under pressure to sell. To do so, they frequently resort to markdowns—a kind of price flexibility.

Printers, on the other hand, have no comparable investment in inventory (mainly paper); furthermore, the paper can be used for a variety of jobs and often can be ordered after a job has been sold. Hence, in printing the pressure of inventory does not encourage flexible prices.

2. Retailers recognize that some goods tie up floor space and sales personnel longer than others. While they do not measure the relevant opportunity costs, they set variable markups on wholesale costs that reflect roughly the differences in opportunity costs.

Printing managers face the problem of estimating opportunity costs. But there is no wholesale cost that could supply a reasonable base for markups; material costs would certainly not provide such a base, since they vary erratically from one job to another. Printers must establish a different base; usually they adopt some measure of chargeable hours on the presses or other processes to which they allocate overhead. In other words, overhead allocation takes the place of a variable markup as an indicator of opportunity costs.

Printers have "an inventory of time," and their accounting methods are designed to provide a rough allocation of the opportunity costs of that time, just as retail markups provide a rough estimate of the opportunity costs of store space. Printing overhead allocations provide a means of rationing time; they help insure that a firm will not schedule orders that interfere with more profitable orders. Retail markups are reversible; if merchandise does not sell, it can be cleared out of the way by price reductions. But printing prices for individual orders are set once and for all, and no price reduction would clear space for other business.

Why, then, are printers more inflexible in insisting on the recovery of the full cost of each job? We have suggested several reasons. They are concerned with allocation of future space rather than the sale of present inventories. Furthermore, they are probably influenced by the "mythology of costs." Full costs appear to be something solid and substantial that should not be compromised; a markup, on the other hand, is something projected out "into the air" that can easily be adapted to circumstances.

Market characteristics

It might also be possible to explain the differences in decision-making procedures from industry to industry in terms of market characteristics. If, for example, oligopoly were more characteristic of printing than of nurseries or retailing, this might help explain the attention to full costs. But such is not the case. In all three industries there is a mixture of market characteristics. Some of the printers operate in large cities and compete in a national market on part of their business; the wholesale nurseries also operate in a national market, while some of the retailers face competition from a fairly large number of firms. At the other extreme, one of the printers in this study faces only one competitor in a small town; there are also cases of both nurseries and retailers facing limited numbers of competitors.

Similarly, there is the same problem of complementarity of demand in each of the three industries. The sales of one product influence the sales of others; present products and prices affect the company "image" and customer goodwill. Printers differ in one respect in dealing with the market; they send salesmen into the market instead of waiting for customers to arrive; these salesmen must be provided with standards for pricing, giving another reason for the emphasis on full costs.

In short, the different status of accounting in decision making in the three industries appears to be based more on production characteristics and on the conventions of management than on market conditions.

IMPLICATIONS FOR PRACTICE

In general, printers use programed accounting methods for pricing and *ad hoc* analyses for other decisions. Is there any reason for them to change this pattern?

1. Full costs provide a convenient starting point in pricing; we have presented several arguments favoring the routinization of cost estimates for pricing in printing. But printers may rely too heavily on full costs, applying them in market situations where greater flexibility is warranted. In any case, printers should not expect too much success from their efforts to stabilize industrywide prices through adoption of common accounting procedures; the industry is too competitive, except in some specialized local markets, to permit this type of price control to work.

2. Small printers have much to gain from a fuller development of cost control systems that provide signals indicating costs that are out of line. Such controls would help indicate areas in which there is a need for decision making.

3. Printers must continue to rely heavily on *ad hoc* analyses, both for pricing situations in which full-cost estimates are not appropriate and for investment, make or buy, and other types of decisions. Perhaps they should give some attention to new quantitative methods of organizing information for decisions, but they must continue to use considerable subjective judgment.

4. Many printers could profit from greater attention to the incremental, discounting, and opportunity cost principles in their *ad hoc* analyses, making certain that they adapt the concepts and measurements to the problems at hand.

In conclusion, there is much to be said for the routinized accounting methods that are being developed in the printing industry, especially for control and pricing. There is, however, a danger that management may be unduly influenced by the full-cost data supplied by such methods, failing to approach special decision-making problems with the full flexibility of analysis required.

6

CASE STUDIES OF
INCREMENTAL ANALYSIS

IN THIS chapter we undertake a more direct discussion of incremental analysis, covering cases not included in previous chapters. Incremental reasoning is quite simple to apply; it is understandable and strongly rooted in commonsense. But it does not offer a panacea for the inherent uncertainties of a dynamic business world.

The incremental principle discussed in Chapter 1 states that a course of action is sound if expected added revenue exceeds expected added cost. We believe that estimates of such changes in costs and revenues are easy to make, once the basic principles are understood. They involve less difficulty than the estimation of average costs, which requires conjectural and arbitrary allocations of overhead. The correct application of this principle, however, does require skill in evaluating the total situation—in recognizing the appropriate opportunity costs and in applying the discounting principle when it is relevant.

DECISION ONE: SIMPLE INCREMENTAL ANALYSIS

Ajax Cleaners is one of several dry cleaning and laundry outlets which are owned by a family corporation that maintains accounting reports for each of the several branches. Mostly, the individual managers are allowed to make their own decisions. But at times the president of the corporation does make suggestions.

In June, 1959, wages and salaries of Ajax were 49 percent of sales, a condition which violated a 33⅓ percent limit.[1] Upon noting this, the president advised the manager to discontinue the shirt laundry (a minor segment of revenue, dry cleaning being the principal service) until November. This suggestion was based on the presumed escapability of labor cost resulting from cessation of the shirt laundry. The final decision was left to the manager; it is his analysis that we evaluate.

The analysis: incremental costs

The manager did not have accounting information in a form needed to resolve the issue. The accounting report received from the central office showed only total costs and revenues classified in major categories. The manager was not furnished with cost and revenue data for purposes other than financial reporting; he had to construct his own decision-making data.

[1] This rule was accepted by the managements of several laundry and dry cleaning firms interviewed during the course of the study. This case illustrates the danger of using such ratios in decision making without analyzing the total situation.

During the month of July he kept an accurate record of costs and revenues which resulted directly from shirt laundry business. Two costs were included in the analysis: labor and supplies. Both were variable costs; both could be avoided when there was no laundry work. Supplies included the soap, water, starch, bleach, packaging, etc., required to launder a "batch" of shirts. Notice that fixed costs were not included—no arbitrary allocations were made. The manager was interested only in the incremental cost of laundering shirts; fixed costs were not relevant for this particular decision.

At the end of July the manager tabulated incremental cost and incremental revenue and compared:

Incremental revenue	$ 740
Incremental cost	390
Net incremental revenue	$ 350

This analysis indicated that if the shirt laundry had been abandoned, net profit for July would have been approximately $350 less than the reported $900. That is, the firm would have escaped from $390 in cost, but at the same time it would have given up $740 in revenue. It is also interesting that the recommended course of action would have reduced the ratio of salaries to sales by one percentage point, but it would have cost the firm *$350!*

The incremental analysis convinced the president that continuation of the shirt laundry was profitable.

An alternative analysis: full costs

Now suppose that incremental analysis had not been used. Assume that full costs were calculated and compared with revenue thusly:[2]

Revenue	$ 740
Full cost	745
"Loss"	$ 5

[2] This calculation, prepared by the interviewer, is based on analysis of income statements and allocation of overhead according to reasonable bases.

Although the "loss" is insignificant in absolute amount, it might have had an influence on the decision. Quite different results would have been obtained from using total costs rather than incremental costs.

This full cost analysis not only suggests that inescapable fixed costs could be escaped; it also ignores the problem of complementarity of demand. Discontinuance of the shirt business might have diminished the cleaning revenues. The incremental point of view, by stressing estimation of all impacts of a decision, is more likely to give attention to such additional changes in revenue.

The decision horizon

The manager's decision was shortrun in character. The laundry was to be suspended only for the summer months—usually a slow season for this segment. This particular feature of the situation enabled the decision maker to concentrate on incremental costs without making allowances for other factors.

1. Opportunity costs were negligible. There were no alternative uses for the fixed facilities of the laundry. If the facilities had been useful for other purposes, it would have been important to consider these alternatives.

2. The longrun impact of the decision was negligible. Cessation of the service during the summer months would not have materially affected future shirt laundry business, at least in the opinion of local management.

3. The discounting principle was not important because of the extremely shortrun implications of the decision.

Implications for accounting

Two observations are made concerning the role of accounting in this decision: an accounting report induced the decision; but past this step, accounting data were not used. Decision making of this sort was not a purpose of the accounting system; the purpose was financial reporting for upper echelon control.

A decision of this kind has occurred only once and was easily handled by a special cost study; yet there is justification for programed accounting data. Two services, dry cleaning and shirt laundry, are competing for scarce resources which must be allocated. Slumping profits and unacceptable income statement item relationships caused the existing allocation to be questioned; yet it should be useful for the firm to analyze the "product mix" continually and to effect adjustments in the light of existing conditions. That is, the firm could adopt offensive rather than defensive tactics. To expedite such decisions, management could be furnished with programed data which convey the correct concept of relative profitability—contribution of each segment to fixed costs.

Thus, we can detect good reasons for having programed data of the sort accumulated by the manager for the special study. And there is no reason why both purposes—financial reporting and decision making—cannot be served. The data could easily have been accumulated and summarized according to the format of marginal income analysis.

A note on marginal income analysis

In an earlier chapter we introduced the basic concepts of marginal income analysis. In the preceding section we suggested that the dry cleaning establishment could benefit from the method. At no point have we stated how a firm might design an accounting system which would develop the data systematically. There is literature which indicates how this might be done, but it deals with large organizations having trained staff members.[3] Using as our model the small

[3] See Albert J. Bergfeld, James S. Earley, and William R. Knobloch, *Pricing for Profit and Growth* (New York: McGraw-Hill, 1957); Earley, *Jour. Pol. Econ.*, LXIII, 227-42; National Association of Cost Accountants, *The Analysis of Cost-Profit-Volume Relationships*, N.A.C.A. Research Report (Reprint of Research Series 16, 17, and 18 published in the *N.A.C.A. Bulletin* 1949-50); National Association of Accountants, *Separating and Using Costs as Fixed and Variable*, Accounting Practice Report No. 10, June, 1960, sec. 3. In addition to the above, we must recognize and acknowledge the work done by vari-

cleaning firm, we present here the various steps in the process of developing programed marginal income analysis for a small business.

Determination of relevant segments. A segment may be a product, a product line, or a service. In multiproduct firms, each product or product line is a segment, or contributor to the gross revenues of the firm. In our example, we shall consider two segments—dry cleaning and shirt laundry.

Segregation of costs between fixed and variable. There are three basic means by which costs can be segregated: (1) analysis of the chart of accounts, (2) statistical interpretation of past results, and (3) engineering studies of cost-volume relationships. A recent publication states that statistical analysis is the more popular method in large corporations.[4] The small firm might find it expedient to analyze the chart of accounts and, under various assumptions of change in output of a segment, to estimate the change in individual costs. The firm might do as the manager of the firm above did: actually observe and record the variable costs incurred in a segment.

There are many woolly questions in cost studies of this kind. Probably the greatest problem is segregating fixed from variable costs. Few costs are wholly fixed or wholly variable; some costs increase discontinuously with the output of a segment. But there are certain useful guides for making the segregation.

1. *Assigned fixed costs* of a segment include only those costs which are "fixed" for shortrun operations, but which can be avoided if the segment is permanently discontinued. Depreciation of special equipment as well as the salaries of supervisors or key employees are obvious examples.[5]

---

ous trade associations. The American Institute of Laundering, Joliet, Illinois, for example, has encouraged members to recognize the usefulness of fixed-variable cost segregation in decision making.

[4] *Separating and Using Costs as Fixed and Variable*, p. 11.

[5] If there is no market for the equipment, then depreciation cannot be avoided.

2. *Variable costs* of a segment include costs that vary with output of the segment. Obviously, it is necessary to compromise between precision and practicality. In few instances will there be a continuous relationship; rather discontinuity characterizes the usual relationship between cost and output. A special study of costs in each segment can reveal the costs which do vary over a relevant range of output.

3. *Unassigned fixed costs* include those costs which do not vary with the output of a segment and which could not be avoided by a permanent retrenchment of any one segment.

Development of a system of accounts. A study has been made of the variability of costs in the two segments of the dry cleaning and laundry case. On this basis, a chart of accounts is established which facilitates reporting to management.

Four major classifications of accounts with various sub-accounts are needed.[6]

Laundry
1. Sales Revenue
2. Variable Costs
   (a) Wages
   (b) Supplies
   (c) Heat, light, power
   (d) Employer's payroll tax
   (e) Repair and maintenance
   (f) Clothes lost and repaired
3. Assigned fixed costs
   (a) Depreciation of equipment

Dry Cleaning
1. Sales Revenue
2. Variable Costs
   (a) Wages
   (b) Supplies
   (c) Heat, light, power
   (d) Employer's payroll tax
   (e) Repair and maintenance
   (f) Clothes lost and repaired
3. Assigned fixed costs
   (a) Depreciation of equipment

4. Unassigned fixed costs
   (a) Salaries
   (b) Advertising

[6] The discussion from this point on is based on analysis of income statements of the firm. We have made a number of assumptions which could be checked by a closer study of the firm's operations.

(c) Repairs and maintenance of plant
(d) Taxes
(e) Telephone
(f) Heat, light, power
(g) Employer's payroll tax
(h) Rent
(i) Depreciation of building, fixtures
(j) Amortization of leasehold improvements
(k) Insurance

Some salaries and wages, such as the manager's and receiving clerk's, are fixed and not affected by the output of the two segments; others, such as an unskilled pressman's, vary with the output. There may be movement of the labor force between the two segments; this is not a problem because of the firm's ability to cut back labor whenever there is no work.

Heat, light, and power costs must be studied to determine the extent to which each can be attributed to the two segments. Some of the cost is attributable to neither (both segments are under the same roof) and therefore must be classified as unassigned fixed cost.

After the account classification is established, financial data are recorded in the usual manner. At regular intervals the accounts are summarized and reports prepared, which then must be interpreted by management. The last step then is to use the reports correctly.

Interpretation of the reports. Figure 4 illustrates the kind of income statement that might have been received by the firm for June, 1959, had a marginal income accounting system been used. This report would have indicated that it would not have been advisable to discontinue the shirt laundry. The segment is contributing a positive sum to the unassigned cost. On this basis, there is no justification for the president's suggested course of action.

Even if the firm recognizes the importance of demand considerations and even if it realizes that incremental analysis does not mean prices should be set at incremental costs, there are real dangers in any system which depends upon

Figure 4. An income statement resulting from a programed marginal income analysis accounting system

	Dry Cleaning		Laundry		
Sales		$2,800		$480	
Variable cost:					
Wages	$790		$170		
Supplies	760		136		
Heat, light, power	150		25		
Employer's payroll tax	43		9		
		1,743		340	
Contribution to assigned and unassigned fixed cost		$1,057		$140	
Depreciation		200		100	
Contribution to unassigned fixed cost		$ 857		$ 40	$ 897
Unassigned fixed cost:					
Salaries		$650			
Advertising		88			
Telephone		66			
Heat, light, power		35			
Employer's payroll tax		36			
Rent		100			
Depreciation		183			
Amortization		140			
Insurance		95			
					1,393
Net loss for the period					$ 496

relations that change with time. There is an ever-present danger that what may have been a variable cost at the time the account classification was established has reverted to a fixed cost when the time comes to make a decision.[7] This problem can never be completely eliminated; yet, by continually examining the classification in terms of what is known to be true at the present, corrections can be made.

A second danger is that the information is not relevant for *all* decisions—as indeed is true of any one source of data. But for a great number of functions, e.g., short-term budgeting, selective selling, product selection, and pricing, this information can be useful.

In spite of these difficulties, marginal income analysis is complementary to incremental analysis: it emphasizes *changes* in cost in response to a controllable factor—output. It is not a substitute for the management function but can be a valuable adjunct.

DECISION TWO: COMPLEX INCREMENTAL ANALYSIS

Steven's Tire Company is located in a large metropolitan area. In years past, 75 percent of total revenue resulted from wholesale orders, and 25 percent resulted from retail sales. In 1959, the firm was stimulated to search for ways of increasing profits, which had dropped $15,000 since 1957.

Immediate action

To counter the trend of diminishing profits, the firm undertook an extensive advertising campaign. The objective of the strategy was to increase retail sales of tires. Although the bulk of the firm's business was wholesale trade, retail sales were more profitable per individual order. There were no evident results from the advertising campaign, and the firm considered actions with longer range effects.

[7] For example, the variable wage of an unskilled employee may become an unavoidable salary as he gains skill as a pressman. If so, his payment must be reclassified as an assigned fixed cost.

Long-range action

Three alternatives were considered by the firm when the downward trend in profits was not arrested by the immediate action: (1) to purchase rental property, (2) to establish an additional retail outlet, and (3) to purchase new equipment. Only the first and second alternatives were seriously considered; general improvement in technology was expected in a few years which would render obsolete any equipment purchased at that time. The decision maker chose to purchase rental property; the process by which this course was selected is of particular interest.

The firm found a possible site which could be leased for $3,000 per annum. An estimate of incremental costs was prepared by the interviewer which included the salary of a salesman and bookkeeper and other operating expenses. The labor force would be supplemented by transferring two men from the present shop to the new location; their salaries would not be incremental. Additionally, one of the three executives would have to devote his full time to the new store; this would not involve an added cash expenditure. The estimate of incremental net revenues was:

Expected annual revenue from new location		$ 88,000
Less: Incremental cost of goods sold	$ 66,000	
Incremental operating expenses	12,550	78,550
Net incremental revenue		$ 9,450

The computation indicates that the decision would be quite lucrative, especially since the initial investment was only $2,000 (office furniture and fixtures, depreciation of which was included in the calculation of incremental costs). The proposal seems even more appealing when it is recognized that the capitalized present value of the investment is about $28,000.[8] In other words, for $2,000 the firm could purchase

[8] This figure was not calculated by the firm. The five-year discount period was chosen because it seems reasonable in terms of the situation. The discount rate is likewise an arbitrary choice, although 20 percent does allow for the uncertainty involved by heavily discounting revenue in the last two years.

an asset with a present worth of better than fourteen times its cost. Why then was this alternative not chosen? Let us look at the analysis of the alternative before answering that question.

The firm had been purchasing property near its present location, which was to have provided space for expected expansion. Yet the expected growth did not materialize and the firm found itself in the position of landlord of two apartment houses. The opportunity arose during the time the retail outlet was being considered to purchase the remaining building on the block. The final price quoted and accepted was $11,500. The firm estimated that net rental income would be approximately $1,900; the building would pay out in about six years, well within the ten-year pay-back criterion that the firm considered appropriate for rental property.

The firm expected that within ten years this property would be sold at an appreciated value; urban redevelopment projects were being talked of for this area. On the basis of this information, we estimate the present value to be about $16,000, well in excess of the cost ($11,500).[9]

We do not claim much for the exactness of our present value calculations, nor do we intend to make an issue of the fact that, according to our estimates, the retail store appears to be the more profitable alternative. Let us, instead, evaluate the reasons the firm gave for choosing the rental property.

The bases for the choice

First, regarding the retail outlet, the principal concern of the firm was the strain such a move would have on management. The executive that the firm would transfer to the new store was, in large measure, responsible for servicing a number of wholesale accounts. It appeared that the sales

[9] We chose to use a ten-year period and 10 percent discount rate; the tenth year includes $12,000 for the sale of the building and $1,900 for rent.

101

to these accounts would suffer should he transfer. In economic terms, there was an opportunity cost involved which should be charged to the new store.

Another opportunity cost was the *possibility* that with the sales executive absent, it might be necessary to hire a wholesale sales manager at a salary of $100 per week. This contingency, though not quantitatively expressed, carried a heavy subjective penalty.

Secondly, profits were improving during the period of the analysis. Thus the objective which the firm had sought to attain was satisfied; there was no longer reason to undertake drastic measures.

One can understand why the firm might choose the rental property in lieu of the retail outlet. We do not have a clear explanation as to why *both* proposals were not accepted; present value, it is safe to say, exceeded the cost of both investment proposals. The fact is that management did not give full attention to the retail store opportunity and let it go by default.

Evaluation

The management of Steven's Tire Company did not completely analyze the retail store alternative; therefore, it is difficult to evaluate the decision-making processes. But we have indicated that incremental analysis would have focused attention on the relevant variables. The opportunity costs were difficult to measure and the demand for management's attention to routine matters did not encourage more serious attention to their measurement. Thus it appears that the complexities of the decision accompanied by the dearth of management time to unravel the complexities prevented full exploitation of the situation.

In conclusion, incremental analysis would have been appropriate for this decision problem, but this does not mean that the whole analysis could have been quantified. In fact, we have indicated that subjective evaluations of opportunity costs would have been required.

102

The decision and its implications for accounting

This discussion has indicated the failure of accounting to provide information on the relevant costs of a decision. We are in no position, however, to criticize the accounting system on this score; its obvious purpose in the organization was for financial reporting and, in some respects, cost control. It is doubtful that any form of accounting data would produce the correct cost figures for decisions of the type confronted by Steven's Tire Company. The case study demonstrates the limitations of any programed approach, including marginal income analysis; programed methods are incapable of taking into account the special circumstances of all available alternatives.

SELECTED CASE STUDIES

The following brief cases compare actual analysis with incremental analysis and also show the bearing which accounting data have or might have to the situation.

1. A decision to purchase a truck for daily service to supermarket wine departments

Actual analysis. A subjective analysis was made by a wine distributor comparing the additional costs of operating a truck with the additional revenues resulting from the better service. Overhead was not allocated to this new "source" of revenue, nor was the cost of the driver included—he was already on the payroll and would be transferred to the new job. His former duties could be handled by other employees.

Incremental analysis. Not much can be added to the actual analysis except to note that implicit interest was not charged to the truck. Even though internal funds were used to purchase the truck, interest should have been included to give recognition to opportunity costs. This would have in no way affected the outcome of the decision, since the amount of money involved was not material.

Implications for accounting. Accounting data could

have been used in this decision only to indicate the whole-sale cost of additional wine. Other costs had to be estimated or secured from other sources.

2. A *decision to sell a standard product at a reduced price*

Actual analysis. A clay refractory received an offer from a distant customer to take a product during the off season at a reduced price. The firm accepted the offer, since the additional revenue from this contract would greatly exceed the incremental cost of the product. The firm did not allocate overhead for this decision; rather it considered only the added cost required to produce the desired quantity—variable costs.

It was recognized that this price concession would in no way affect other business, and there was no indication of possible, more lucrative, offers.

Incremental analysis. This case is a straightforward example of the application of incremental analysis. Indeed, it seems so elementary that one might question its inclusion. Yet the following case (No. 3) is parallel in every respect except that a different course of action was taken.

Implications for accounting. The firm had to estimate the incremental cost of this product. The accounting system developed only total costs, from which average costs were estimated. Variable costing would have given the firm an indication of the relevant cost for this decision.

3. A *decision to sell a standard service at a reduced price*

Actual analysis. A laundry establishment regularly bid on special business (motel and hotel contracts for "flat work") during the summer months in order to fill excess capacity. Yet in formulating the bid, the firm would never go below "full cost." This extra off-season business would in no way affect future business and there was no more profitable use of the idle capacity; the firm consistently lost these contracts by refusing to bid below full cost.

Incremental analysis. In view of the circumstances, the

104

only cost that was relevant for this decision was the additional cost of doing the business. Overhead was an irrelevant cost. If a bid was accepted which covered the incremental cost of the business and made some contribution to overhead, it would have been profitable. Yet management desired that all business cover full cost—and profits probably suffered as a result of the policy.

Implications for accounting. While managers cannot be expected to use cost data which they consider "wrong," sound handling of this decision would have considered the kind of data developed by marginal income analysis.

4. A decision to sell home-cooked foods on a percentage of sales arrangement

Actual analysis. The firm, a small gift shop, considered only the revenues that might result from the sale of the food. There was no merchandise cost, and the producers took back all leftovers. No overhead was allocated. The additional sales of other items that might result from handling food were considered important. No doubt customers were attracted who would have gone elsewhere to buy the gifts and dry goods sold by this store. The management recognized that no additional sales force was required to handle these foods.

Incremental analysis. The analysis of this firm proceeded correctly, except that the opportunity cost of alternative use of the shelf space was not formally considered. Although this case is seemingly rather simple, we might mention that a similar firm discontinued the product because it was suspected of not paying for its overhead.

Implications for accounting. It is doubtful that any kind of accounting data would help in this kind of decision, except to report sales of the item to enable periodic comparison with alternatives. The estimation of the impact of home-cooked food on other sales was necessarily subjective; accounting would have had nothing to contribute to such an analysis.

105

5. A decision to buy a component part of a finished product instead of making it

Actual analysis. The analysis of this manufacturer proceeded by comparing the variable cost of making the part with the purchase price (including estimated costs of receiving and stocking the part). Yet the analysis ceased to be incremental when the firm reallocated the overhead to other processes; higher unit costs resulted which indicated that higher prices would have to be charged on other finished products. On these grounds, the decision was to continue making the part.

Incremental analysis. Had the firm considered *escapable* costs to be the only relevant cost concept, it might not have handled the problem in the way that it did. As long as the cost of buying from an outside supplier exceeded the escapable costs, it was advantageous to make the part rather than to buy it. The reallocation of overhead was unnecessary and irrelevant.

Implications for accounting. The results of this decision indicate clearly the danger of wrongly using overhead allocations. Incidents such as these present strong arguments in favor of direct costing, although this would do no good unless management accepts the validity of incremental concepts.

6. A decision to install an inventory of men's suits to replace a "made to measure" arrangement with a distant factory

Actual analysis. A small men's shop had a "made to measure" arrangement requiring no inventory of suits; customers were measured and specifications sent to the factory, which made the suits accordingly. On these sales the firm received 45 percent of the selling price. A supplier offered the firm a line of suits with a national reputation, but at a 35 percent gross profit. The proposal was rejected on two grounds: the required inventory investment and the lower markup. No real evaluation was made of opportunity costs.

106

Incremental analysis. Other factors should have been considered in the decision. Incremental revenues should include estimates of total revenue from the sale of suits and other items which might be sold because of complementary demand. From these revenues, estimated incremental costs would be subtracted: (1) lost revenue from abandonment of "made to measure" suits; (2) additional costs incurred because of the new suits, including handling, advertising, interest on inventory investment, cost of merchandise, etc., but no overhead; (3) estimated profits from alternative uses of the funds (although the interest charge may be sufficient for this purpose).

Of course these estimates would be highly conjectural and may not have changed the decision; the point is the actual analysis did not consider *all* the relevant costs.

Implications for accounting. Accounting data could not possibly have indicated the opportunity costs involved in this decision. The *concepts* of merchandise management accounting could have been used, although it is doubtful whether a firm of this size could afford to develop more refined data.

7. *A decision on the price of two products, the demand for which appears insensitive to price increases*

Actual analysis. This firm, a small machine shop and metals warehouse, has a price policy which considers a 100 percent markup on cost to be appropriate. The firm is the sole supplier of bronze and stainless steel in the area and there is every indication that the firm could charge higher prices without a loss of business. The cost-plus formula does not permit demand-orientated pricing.

Incremental analysis. If we assume that the firm wishes to maximize profits, then we should expect that it would raise price to garner the additional revenue. This would be the approach of incremental analysis. Other cases may have left the reader with an idea that incremental analysis always means a low price policy, but this is not true. Rather, demand is always a consideration, especially the concept of elasticity of demand.

Implications for accounting. Accounting data can tell little about elasticity of demand. Some indication of future demand might be obtained from past records if the firm has experimented with price in the past; but when this has not been the case, the decision must rest on other sources of data.

CONCLUSIONS

Undoubtedly the principal deterrent of the more general use of incremental analysis is a concept of cost, fostered to some extent by accounting, which managers believe absolute and, consequently, applicable to all decisions. A British accountant, D. R. C. Halford, writing recently, disproves the validity of "the" cost for decision making, and our case studies bear out his conclusion.[10] For the decision maker, cost and revenue must be considered within a flexible framework and properly balanced only after a careful weighing of many factors.

This criticism of the programed system built around full costs should not be taken as criticism of any programed data, nor even of the concept of full cost itself; rather it is directed at the blind acceptance of data. Incremental analysis may make use of programed data, but only if data are accumulated by cause. And the emphasis of incremental methods is not so much on the accumulation of data as upon use and meaning.

What incremental analysis demonstrates and what the case studies of this chapter support is the need for flexibility of cost analyses, with adaptation of cost measurements to particular problems. Therefore, many small firms may profit from learning about incremental reasoning in general, with a resultant improvement in their *ad hoc* decision making. It

[10] D. R. C. Halford, *Differential Costs and Management Decisions* (London: Sir Isaac Pitman and Sons, Ltd., 1959), p. 2.

is impossible to say generally when programed incremental analysis is justified. It is possible, however, to state that incremental reasoning, whether programed or nonprogramed, whether subjective or empirical, is necessary for sound decision making.

7

AN OVERVIEW OF INVESTMENT
AND PRICING DECISIONS

*T*HE CENTRAL purpose of this study is to evaluate the role of accounting in the decisions of small firms. We do not concentrate on particular kinds of decisions; rather, we examine a number of different types within the context of particular industries. In this chapter, however, we emphasize two particularly crucial matters in small firms—investment and pricing decisions.

This chapter serves two purposes. One is to bring together in one place the analysis of investment and pricing decisions, which up to this point has been scattered over a series of chapters.[1] The second is to formulate general conclusions on the import of accounting data in these decisions.

INVESTMENT DECISIONS OF SMALL FIRMS

Investment decisions are highly diverse, but they all have two qualities in common: the outlay of funds for new assets and the hope for a return.[2] The focal point is the relationship between *present* expenditures and *future* receipts. The decision maker must estimate whether profits will result in amounts adequate to justify the expenditure. But this is only one step in the process of investment decisions. Effective capital budgeting requires a search for opportunities and a search for information. It entails a forecast of available funds and of the cost of these funds. It implies a rationing of funds to alternatives ranked according to some criterion. It involves a follow-up of previous investments to help evaluate past performance and to improve future decisions. It is not surprising that accounting plays a limited role in investment decisions, for accounting normally provides no information on future receipts or on the availability and cost of funds. Accounting might provide incremental cost and follow-up data. The question is the extent to which the accounting systems of small firms actually provide such data.

Quantitative methods for ranking

Quantitative methods attempt to substitute objective criteria for the more nebulous subjective evaluation of the decision maker. They cannot completely eliminate personal judgment.

Discounted rate of return or present value. These methods are widely accepted as theoretically correct. They

---

[1] For full analyses, see Martin B. Solomon, Jr., *Investment Decisions in Small Business* (Lexington: University of Kentucky Press, 1963); W. Warren Haynes, *Pricing Decisions in Small Business* (Lexington: University of Kentucky Press, 1962).

[2] Ronello B. Lewis, "The Role of Accounting in Decision-Making," *Accounting Review*, XXXV (Jan., 1960), 37.

both involve mathematical techniques based on the discounting principle. Any alternative methods which do not include discounting must be considered as approximations to the true rate of return.

There are difficulties in the practical application of these methods. There is, for example, the problem not only of forecasting the inflows over the length of life of the asset, but also of determining the actual life. Inherent in both is the problem of uncertainty. On the practical level, in view of the uncertain estimates of future data how much precision is lost by using alternative methods? These optional methods are discussed below.

Payback period. This method does not calculate a return on investment, although this characteristic is not always recognized in the literature.[3] The payback period measures only the length of time required for the proposal to return the initial outlay. The calculation is relatively simple: total investment divided by the estimated annual net profit. We see immediately that this method ignores how long the returns will be earned on the investment. It is certainly possible to think of situations in which the payback period is shorter for A than B, yet B may be more profitable because of the longer period of time in which profits accrue. On the other hand, it may be quite reasonable for some firms to demand a quick return of investment due to stringency of funds or great uncertainty about the future. Thus it appears that the use of payback period calculations could result in decisions quite different from those based on the discounted rate of return.

Payback reciprocal. The inverse of the payback period is the payback reciprocal. For projects with a length of life considerably beyond the payback period, this method may give a good approximation of the discounted rate of return.[4]

[3] See James H. Miller, "A Glimpse at Practice in Calculating and Using Return on Investment," N.A.A. *Bulletin*, XLI (June, 1960), 65.
[4] Myron J. Gordon, "The Payoff Period and the Rate of Return," *Journal of Business*, XXVIII (Oct., 1955), 253-60.

But when the length of life is not much greater, the payback reciprocal is an overstatement. It is possible to determine the true rate of return quickly from the payback reciprocal by special tables.[5] Decisions made on the basis of the payback reciprocal alone, however, run the risk of error.

Rate of income on investment. This method, sometimes called the financial statement method, relates the expected revenue of an asset to the cost of that asset without regard to the discounted values or to the fact that revenues may vary from year to year. The first year net income is usually given as a percentage of either the initial investment or the average investment. The accuracy in estimating rates of return is somewhat limited in that it depends on the length of life of the investment. But for the practical problem of ranking alternatives, the method does an admirable job.[6]

Method of analysis employed by some small firms

Of the four quantitative methods, the rate of income on investment is best known to accountants. However, they have shown a growing interest in the other three. In the actual case studies covered by this study, the payback method was the only quantitative method used, aside from one firm which computed the rate of income on investment. These small firms paid little attention to the refinements of quantitative analysis.

A prime consideration in most cases was the requirement that the investment pay out in a short time. Firms did not usually compute the payback period but apparently operated on the principle that investments paying off rapidly were more likely to be profitable.

The rationale for payback and rate of income

We have seen that most small firms do not bother with

---

[5] For example, see National Association of Accountants, *Return on Investment as a Guide to Managerial Decisions*, N.A.A. Research Report No. 35, Dec., 1959, p. 77.

[6] See Solomon.

the refinements of the discounted rate of return or present value. Would they be better off to do so? It is unlikely that such refinements would produce benefits that exceed the added costs in terms of management time and training. The case studies suggest degrees of uncertainty and errors in estimates that would overshadow the significance of any refinements. Even under conditions of certainty the rate of income ranks very well when compared with the discounted rate of return and present value. Under conditions of uncertainty, when errors of estimate are likely, the rate of income probably produces results insignificantly different from more refined methods.

Managers probably find it difficult to apply the discounted rate of return in actual investment decisions. If the above argument is correct, the rate of income is justified.

The argument for a short payback period raises similar doubts about refinements. Under conditions of financial stringency there is a strong motivation for rapid returns. Also under conditions of great uncertainty it is understandable that stress be placed on the first few years' performance. Short-lived investments provide flexibility, and flexibility is a major objective under uncertain conditions.

The real deficiency of small firms in capital budgeting is not in the area of ranking and choosing. Small firms as represented by this study, with some exceptions, do an admirable job of choosing profitable alternatives. But there is every reason to state that the owners and managers of these same firms might well engage in more intensive search activity, more creative thinking. The small businessman, however, must perform various functions—planning, production scheduling, selling, labor relations, public relations, accounting, etc.—leaving little time for the necessary ingredient of adequate capital budgeting—search. The issue resolves itself into a weighing of cost and revenue. Can the manager reap greater profits by delegating responsibility for routine tasks and thus releasing more time for search activity? Obviously, this issue must be resolved by each small businessman.

114

Implications for accounting

A survey of accounting literature quickly reveals that some accountants have accepted as valid the discounted rate of return and present value analysis. A current research report by the National Association of Accountants indicates strongly that discounted rate of return is more useful and accurate than the financial statement method (rate of income on investment).[7] The report cites Dean on the practicality of the discounted rate of return: "Because the approach is new in this application (capital budgeting) its use requires persuasion and education. Moreover, it initially appears to be complex. But this appearance is deceptive; once the basic method is understood it is actually simpler and quicker to use than the levelbook method."[8] Other accountants accept the theoretical soundness of the method but question its universal practicality. Bierman, for example, says: "It was once hoped that the present value or rate of return techniques would offer simple solutions to the problem of making capital investment decisions. It is now obvious that these decisions are complex and that there is no one, simple, and correct answer to be obtained."[9] There are others who argue that the rate of income on investment is preferable to the discounted rate of return from the standpoint of simplicity. This opinion is well illustrated by Lewis' statement: "Nothing could be simpler than the easy formula of book net profit divided by gross investment to produce rate of return."[10]

On the basis of the case studies, we recognize that the uncertainty inherent in most estimates of future revenues and lengths of life limits the validity of any ranking process based on rate of return or present value analysis. Therefore,

[7] *Return on Investment as a Guide to Managerial Decisions.*

[8] Joel Dean, "Profitability Indexes for Capital Investments," *Controller*, XXXVI (Feb., 1958), 67; quoted in N.A.A. Research Report 35, Dec., 1959, p. 73.

[9] Harold Bierman, Jr., *Managerial Accounting: An Introduction* (New York: Macmillan Co., 1959), p. 435.

[10] Lewis, *Acctg. Rev.*, XXXV, 41.

the effort required to develop these analyses is not usually justified.[11]

Investment decisions require much more information than is divulged by accounting records. Recorded costs are, at best, only an imperfect approximation of costs required for investment decisions; it is necessary to analyze accounting data to determine which are relevant. Small firms must accept the fact that investment decisions require data on future revenues and expenses, costs of capital, and rates of obsolesence, none of which may be supplied from accounting records.

PRICING DECISIONS OF SMALL FIRMS

In the discussion of pricing decisions,[12] the central issues are the extent to which small firms refer to full costs, incremental analysis, and accounting data.

Cost-plus formulas and pricing decisions

That some small firms use cost-plus formulas in making pricing decisions should be no surprise to those who have read other empirical studies on pricing.[13] This pricing policy is followed for many reasons: a sense of "fairness," ignorance of demand conditions, uncertainty of competitors' reactions, assumed low elasticities of demand for price decreases, and the administrative difficulties involved in more flexible price policies. Some firms examined in this study appear to be especially concerned with the effect of pricing on customer goodwill and longrun volume. However, the majority of small firms do not apply full-cost formulas mechanically; they generally relate their prices to demand as well as costs. Thus our findings do not support the conclusions in some

[11] For a fuller development of this argument see Solomon, esp. chap. 6.

[12] Haynes.

[13] Robert L. Hall and Charles J. Hitch, *Price Theory and Business Behavior*, Oxford Economic Papers No. 2, May, 1939, pp. 12, 18-22, 25-27, 29-33.

previous studies that suggest a rigid adherence to predetermined markups on costs.

In many cases, the profit markup varies according to the firms' best estimates of demand. That is, the markup is maintained by the firm only so long as demand allows. In other cases the firms actually reduce their estimates of full cost if, when the markup is applied, the resultant price proves unacceptable in the market. It is most important to recognize that cost-plus pricing is a multistep process in which the initial planned markup may be adjusted through time and tailored to the individual products.

Most small businesses are multiproduct firms and sell their products under diverse market conditions. In some markets and for some products they may have a strong monopoly position; in others, they may face close competition. The evidence shows that these firms adjust prices to the varied conditions rather than follow mechanical pricing rules, thereby demonstrating cross-sectional flexibility on individual products as well as flexibility over time.

Some firms regard full cost as a level below which prices should not fall. They take this stand as a result of considerations of market stability, of customer relations, and of competition. Sometimes they may take it simply because management has failed to recognize a variety of cost concepts, expecting each product to return its share of profits. The policy of "full cost floors" is, in some measure, a compromise accepted by small firms in recognition of the restraints imposed upon them by their size and their closer relationship with their customers.

Full costs are used in some instances in a manner contrary to the economists' prescription for pricing. There are several firms, especially in the printing industry, which staunchly support the notion that every product should bear its share of overhead. We have discussed already the case of a laundry which refused to take a profitable special order at less than full cost. We have also discussed a clay refractory which did recognize the commonsense of accepting a special bid at less than full cost but at more than variable cost. But it is impossible to state generally that small firms either reject or accept marginal reasoning.

To be complete, some mention should be made of firms that avoid pricing decisions. Some firms simply imitate the prices of others. Some follow the suggestions of manufacturers or wholesalers. This is not necessarily contradictory to incremental reasoning; the manufacturers' suggestions probably reflect attention to market forces. There is strong reason for believing that suggested markups recognize differing demand elasticities on various products.[14]

Pricing decisions in many firms are indicative of the ultimate aims of management. A desire for adequate or satisfactory profits is evidenced by the failure of many firms to change prices until they become dissatisfied with the results shown on their income statements. Some firms are not engaged in a constant struggle for maximum profits. Other firms consider maximum profits to be the proper goal. Some firms experiment with price, recognize elasticities of demand, and capitalize on cost-profit-volume analysis.

In those firms which stress full costs in pricing, accounting takes on a great significance. Accounting systems provide estimates of full costs. But as we have seen, full cost estimates are not so important in pricing decisions as they first appear.

One basic conclusion of incremental analysis for pricing is that there are two determinants of price—cost and demand. Practical application of this idea is often hampered by scarce information on demand. The firm has, from experience, some notion of what customers have paid in the past, but this serves as only an approximation of what they would be willing and able to pay in the future.

Incremental analysis considers the response of costs to

---

[14] Two other pricing methods—"gross margin" pricing, and pricing when cost, because of its nebulous character, has little influence—have been discussed. Examples of these instances have been evaluated in earlier chapters and need not be repeated.

changes in volume. For establishing selling prices, only those costs which change with output are relevant: the firm must have variable cost information. The obvious source of such data is the accounting system. But all too often the cost system does not divulge variable cost data explicitly. Rather, the firm must sift through the accounts and anticipate which costs are pertinent. Here the small firm is in a better position than the large firm because management is close enough to operations to estimate the variable costs.

A consequence of incremental analysis is that every product is not required to recover its full cost. This idea has long been recognized in retailing, where we find "loss leaders" and "close out" sales. In other industries this conclusion has not been accepted—thus there may be adherence to "full cost."

It should be repeated that incremental reasoning does not imply low prices. What it does imply is adjustment of prices to both demand and cost influences. A firm that takes advantage of inelastic demand by raising prices far above costs is behaving consistently with incremental reasoning.

It is not suggested that all firms can profit from close attention to pricing. Some of them are probably quite right in concentrating on other types of decisions: advertising, sales promotion, inventory control, product mix, and so on. What is important is that small businesses not fall short of optimum pricing because of failure to recognize the correct concepts.

Implications for accounting

A leading accountant suggests that cost accounting may sometimes bolster management's tendency to price on the basis of full costs.[15] The distribution of overhead may be accepted as a reflection of the relative usage of scarce factors of production, without recognition of differences in contribution to profit.

[15] Devine, *Acctg. Rev.*, XXV, 384-9. Reprinted in Thomas, pp. 333-41.

On the other hand, an economist, James S. Earley, argues that cost accounting has actually had a positive influence in winning acceptance of incremental reasoning. His study finds that "leading cost accountants and management consultants are currently advocating principles of accounting analysis and decision-making that are essentially 'marginalist' in character and implications."[16]

It is difficult to determine, therefore, whether accounting has had a positive or negative influence on adoption of incremental reasoning in pricing. In this study of small firm decisions there has been evidence both of confusion resulting from overhead allocations and of fairly sophisticated use of accounting data. Probably cost accountants are responsible for neither, since few small firms can afford their services. If small businessmen make correct or incorrect use of accounting, it is usually a result of their own training and volition.

A central issue throughout this volume has been the profitability of programed accounting methods in small business pricing decisions. Generally, we have been skeptical of the value of programed incremental data, mainly because small businesses do not have sufficient occasion to use such data. Management is close enough to the situation to make special studies of costs and volume with little effort. Unless management understands the assumptions involved in marginal accounting, it is likely to misapply the results. We have cited cases in which marginal income data would have been useful; it would be desirable if some firms experimented with these new accounting methods. However, as a general statement, *ad hoc* analysis is probably more suitable in most small firms, provided management accepts the underlying reasoning.

[16] James S. Earley, "Marginal Policies of 'Excellently Managed' Companies," *American Economic Review*, XLVI (March, 1956), 44.

8

CONCLUSION

*A*CCOUNTING is one of the greatest factors in motivating management to initiate the decision-making process. Managers commonly have predetermined notions of what constitutes satisfactory accounting results, and if they are dissatisfied with current results, they exhibit a homeostatic tendency to search for improvements. The income statement is particularly important in this respect; if the net income figure falls short of aspirations, new alternatives are sought. Accounting ratios and standards also enable businessmen to compare actual results with those in other firms or with established norms. Many of our cases illustrate the homeostatic role of these ratios and standards.

To turn from description to evaluation, there can be no doubt of the value of accounting in calling attention to deficiencies in the present state of affairs and in motivating management to devote attention to the major issues. A few cases exist in which the accounts deflect attention from the real issues, but in the main the accounts serve a constructive control function. If a need exists in this area, it is to improve the design of accounting systems so as to focus attention on the significant deviations from standards.

THE ASSEMBLY AND ANALYSIS
OF RELEVANT INFORMATION

The present study is primarily concerned with the way in which accounting can and does assemble the kinds of data needed for decisions and the way it organizes the variables required by the logic of decision making. Before we can evaluate the role of accounting in this phase, we must first review the nature of rational choice.

Rational decision-making models

Earlier chapters present models that indicate the kinds of data required for rational decisions. These models incorporate the principles of managerial economics outlined in Chapter 1—the incremental principle, the time perspective principle, the discounting principle, and the opportunity cost principle. They involve much more: consideration of demand elasticities and of market structures; evaluation of the impact of decisions on customer goodwill and on the company "image"; and dozens of factors specific to each problem. A complete mathematical application of such models to business decisions would require that management discover the exact quantitative nature of key relationships: of volume to price, of cost to product mix, of sales today to sales in the future, of the cost of capital, and so on.

It is quite clear that small businessmen cannot obtain the exact quantities needed by such a model; it is even impossible to think simultaneously of all the relationships involved in such a model (and the model is itself a simplification). Small businessmen must focus attention on those variables that appear to be most relevant. In the language of modern management literature, they must "suboptimize" because it costs too much time and effort to "optimize."

In the world of uncertainty the accountant prefers to record the known past and thus avoids the risks of prognostication. Businessmen quite understandably often devote attention to certain but irrelevant data from the past instead of relevant but conjectural estimates for the future. They have a tendency to use the information at hand, and accounting information is especially accessible. Thus businessmen make use of full-cost data, partly because such data give a feeling of solidity, partly because they are the result of widely accepted convention, and partly because they divert attention from the need to look into the complexities of the future.

This tendency to select the known rather than the unknown is not in itself unsound. The uncertainty about the effects of decisions is often so great as to negate the value of refined techniques. The important need is not so much the refined analysis of the alternatives that are known as it is an imaginative search for new and superior alternatives. Neither accounting nor theoretical model building can help the businessman in this search.

Accounting and decision-making models

Accounting at best involves a compromise with the refinements of economic theory and management science. The question then becomes whether the accounting procedures presently used by small firms are the right kind of compromise.

There are some situations in which programed accounting methods provide what appears to be a reasonable adaptation to the problem. The reliance on full costs for pricing in oligopolistic markets may contribute to maintaining customer goodwill and avoiding competitive retaliation. The methods most commonly used by accountants for evaluating investments (sometimes known as the "accountant's method") do about as well as refined methods in ranking investment opportunities in a world of uncertainty.[1] Data produced as a byproduct of financial or cost accounting are inexpensive and are available at regular intervals; they thus provide a convenient starting point for many decisions.

The fact remains that accounting is concerned with the past rather than the future. The question is whether past data can aid in the prediction of future variables and relationships. An outstanding work on decision making suggests that there are five kinds of prediction—*persistence prediction*, when stable characteristics of the data maintain a close relationship between the past and the future; *trajectory prediction*, when past trends promise to persist in the future; *cyclic prediction*, when past patterns repeat themselves; *associative prediction*, when there are persistent correlations among variables; and *analogue prediction*, when a simplified model (mathematical or not) maintains a consistent relation to the real world.[2] Accounting systems can supply raw materials for all of these kinds of prediction. But accounting cannot indicate when the necessary stabilities in the data exist; this is a problem for managerial judgment or for statistical analysis.

As we have seen in some case studies, traditional accounting may at times confuse rather than clarify decision making by focusing attention on the wrong data. The outstanding example is in the measurement of full costs. Full costs do not measure the *change* in costs occasioned by a decision, for they include elements that are not affected by decisions. Economists have long noted the divergence between the accountant's depreciation expense and "economic

[1] The reasoning and empirical evidence underlying this generalization are developed in Solomon.

[2] Irwin J. Bross, *Design for Decision* (New York: Macmillan, 1953), pp. 34-8.

124

depreciation." This is a further illustration of a "cost" that may not be relevant for a particular problem.

We suggest that small businessmen have three choices if they wish to improve their decision making: (1) they can attempt to apply modern quantitative techniques such as linear programing and other refined mathematical models (accounting can supply data for these models); (2) they can supplement regular accounting with special forms of incremental accounting; or (3) they can improve *ad hoc* techniques for dealing with decision making. The first is not feasible for most small firms because of the expense and the special skills required. The others have possibilities worth further comment.

Special forms of incremental accounting

Earlier chapters indicate developments in accounting that move in the direction suggested by the incremental principle. These developments go under various names— direct costing, marginal income analysis, cost-profit-volume analysis, differential cost analysis, merchandise management accounting, and so on. Some small firms might profit from adopting relatively inexpensive forms of marginal income analysis that do not require extensive changes in the traditional accounts; they merely require special statements that reorganize the data already supplied in the accounts.

Marginal income analysis has limitations noted in earlier chapters. It does not meet the need for flexible, "tailor-made" costs. No programed data collection system can provide exactly the kinds of information required for all decisions. Furthermore, marginal income analysis has no use in firms in which management does not accept the incremental logic on which it is built. Nevertheless, one of our major recommendations is for more extensive experimentation with incremental accounting techniques.

Improvement of ad hoc analyses

Small business decision making must continue to rely

heavily on nonprogramed analyses which are adapted to the problem at hand. One need in this area is for more systematic analyses. Many managers devote too little attention to the search for new alternatives and for information about alternatives. Many would benefit from merely organizing their thoughts on paper. Attempts at partial quantification are likely to clarify thought processes, even when it is impossible to measure all the variables.

Many firms would profit from greater attention to external sources of information that could be used in their *ad hoc* analyses. Some might experiment with inexpensive forms of market research; one firm in our study is about to engage in research that should be helpful in locating new markets and in tapping old markets more effectively; the total expense of this project should not exceed $1,500. In addition, there are numerous published sources of data and ideas that most small firms do not exploit to the fullest (examples are cited in Chapter 1).

Throughout this volume we have stressed the importance of a few economic principles relevant to business decisions. We believe that an understanding of these principles, which are little more than a refinement of commonsense, can make a significant contribution to logical *ad hoc* analyses. With the aid of these principles, managers can make adjustments in accounting data to arrive at estimates that have meaning to the particular problem. They can separate the costs that are fixed from those that are incremental; they can combine these cost estimates with whatever demand estimates and discounting rates seem appropriate.

We thus stress several requirements for improved small business decisions—better education in the meaning of the data supplied by the present accounting systems, improved skills in adapting these data to individual decision-making problems, greater attention to the relations between past and future data, recognition of the nonaccounting variables that must be combined with accounting estimates to permit complete analyses, and a fuller recognition of the fundamental economic concepts that are needed for the correct interpretation of the various types of information that are available. There are no mechanical devices or formulas to replace the businessman's own skills in adapting accounting data to his individual problems.

INDEX

Historical costs: emphasized in accounting, 20; in retail stores, 44-46; limitations of, 20

Hitch, C. J.: on full-cost pricing, 116n

Hodgson, Harry: empirical studies in small business, 1n

Holdren, Bob R.: on retail decisions, 51n

Homeostasis: and accounting data, 71; and cost accounting, 8-9; and financial accounting, 7-8, 42-43; in retail store accounting, 42-44

Hour costs: in printing, 75, 76-77

Hunziker, Harold: on cost accounting for nurseries, 30n

Income departmental reporting: in retail stores, 55

Income statement: homeostatic function of, 7-8; influence of in nursery decisions, 25-26; related to decision making, 121

Incremental analysis: and make or buy decisions, 106; and pricing decisions, 118-19; applied in clay refractory case, 104; applied in gift shop case, 105; applied in laundry case, 105; applied in men's clothing store, 107; applied in tire case, 100-102; applied in truck purchase case, 103; case studies in, 90-109; in machine shop case, 107-108; supported, 108-109

Incremental costs: consideration in pricing, 65-66; in laundry decision, 91-92; in nursery decisions, 34-35; in printing, 81; in retailing, 52-53

Incremental reasoning: described, 15-16; in retail decisions, 49, 51

Industry comparisons: with regard to accounting and decision making, 84-88

Investment decisions: discussion of, 110-16; in manufacturing, 57, 61-63; in printing, 71-72, 79

Jardine, Peter: empirical studies in small business, 1n

Jones, Robert I.: on merchandise management accounting, 13n

Knobloch, W. R.: on marginal income analysis, 94n

Leverenz, E. T.: on accounting methods in printing, 76

Lewis, R. B.: on investment decisions, 111n, 115n

Liquidation decision: study of, 84

Littleton, A. C.: on overhead allocations, 66n

Longrun effects: consideration in decision making, 16

Make or buy decisions: in manufacturing firm, 106; in printing, 79-80

March, J. G.: on search in decision making, 59n

Markups: in printing, 82; in retailing, 43; relation to demand, 117

Managerial economics: important principles of, 15-18; relevance of in decision making, 4, 14-15

Manufacturing firms: case studies in, 57-66; decisions in, 56-69

Marginal income analysis: appropriate for manufacturing decisions, 68; described, 11; evaluated, 125; illustration of, 94-98; in retail stores, 55

Market characteristics: and influence on decision making, 87-88

McNair, M. P., and E. G. May: on merchandise decisions, 49n; on merchandise management accounting, 13n

Merchandise budget: in retail decisions, 46-48, 54

Merchandise management accounting: and incremental reasoning, 13

Miller, J. H.: on payback analysis, 112n

131